SINBAD'S

guide to
Life

[because I know everything]

SINBAD

with

David Ritz

Bantam Books
New York Toronto London Sydney Auckland

This edition contains the complete text
of the original hardcover edition.
NOT ONE WORD HAS BEEN OMITTED.

SINBAD'S GUIDE TO LIFE
A Bantam Book

PUBLISHING HISTORY
Bantam hardcover edition published / June 1997
Bantam paperback edition / April 1998

ISBN 0-553-57592-9

Published simultaneously in the United States and Canada

Bantam Books are published by Bantam Books, a division of
Bantam Doubleday Dell Publishing Group, Inc. Its trademark,
consisting of the words "Bantam Books" and the portrayal of a
rooster, is Registered in U.S. Patent and Trademark Office and in
other countries. Marca Registrada. Bantam Books, 1540 Broadway,
New York, New York 10036.

PRINTED IN THE UNITED STATES OF AMERICA

OPM   10 9 8 7 6 5 4 3 2 1

To every goofy, uncool kid out there somewhere in the world. Remember, hang in there. It's going to be all right.

This book is also dedicated to my parents, Louise and Rev. Dr. Donald Adkins, Sr.; to my brothers, Michael, Donald, Jr., and Mark; and my sisters, Dorothea and Donna (and Dylan, her son); and to my children and partners in crime, Paige and Royce—all of whom never thought for a moment that I was uncool.

Just strange.

Contents

Acknowledgments

I would like to thank Irwyn Applebaum for ever thinking that someone would read a book by me. That's if he's not locked up in a mental institution yet, because we really pushed this book to the wire. Anyone can bring in a book on time, Irwyn. It takes a real man to jump over the fence. I would like to thank Elisa Petrini, for hours and trips, coffee and chips, and for putting up with my on-line chatter—sorry, I'm addicted; David Ritz, the only man with more CDs than me and the funkiest white boy I know—we finally did it, you are *the man;* Kathleen Oga, for your lightning licks on the transcriber—we're going to work again, girl; my staff and crew at David and Goliath Productions for telling me, "You've got to finish this book— you already got the check"; and everyone at Bantam Books.

I am also grateful to all the cool people who took the time to help me smooth out the rough edges, who saw beneath the surface and kept telling me, "Don't change, what you've got is right." And to all those who told me to give up because I didn't have the ability; you made me work harder than I would have on my own. I'm not mad at you.

The Only Man Who Could Ever Teach You . . .

I know what you're thinking: Who does he think he is —"the only man who could ever teach you"? Well, it's from a song: "The only one who could ever teach me was the son of a preacher man . . ."

Now, I am the son of a preacher man, and that was supposed to be the title. But it's too long. The publisher broke down the economics of it for me: The cost of ink and printing it adds up—four extra words can add up to $4 billion. So I had to shorten it up.

Do me a favor now: Look at the cover of this book. What's different? Yeah, that's right—it isn't O.J.! There's a black man on the cover of this book who isn't O.J.! This is the first book like that in years—it took the publishers a little while to buy another brother— and you've got it in your hands. I'm proud of you!

All right now—on to the book! I know you're wondering, "What kind of crazy stuff is Sinbad talking about now? What could Sinbad possibly write about that would help me? Well, the fact is, Mr. or Miss Know-Everything, this book can set you straight in life. How do I know? Because *I do know everything*. And it hurts my head sometimes to carry it all around. In fact, that's the real reason I wanted to write this book, so that I could get a lot of the old information about life that I know down on paper, so that I could forget some of that stuff and make room in my head for all the vital new information that's out there, like on-line E-mail addresses, URLs, and other cool cyberspace stuff. Because that is the future: We aren't going to live in the real world, we're going to live on-line. I've got to get ready for that.

Don't let the idea of my "guide to life" make you think that I'm laying some heavy reading trip on you. I realize the last book you probably read straight through was the instruction book to your VCR and I'm sure the clock on it is still flashing 12:00, so I have tried to make it easy reading for you. I've kept the chapters short so you can take breaks, go to the bathroom, have a life, and be with your family. In fact, this book is best read during bathroom sessions, so you can come to it in complete silence and with total concentration. Don't act like you don't know what I mean. You do read in the bathroom. We've all been there.

And don't confuse this book with those "self-improvement" books they sell on those crazy late-night TV infomercials that tell you how to set fire to your abs or clean everything with one product that you can also brush your teeth with—I don't think so.

Also, do not look for this book to feed your addiction

to daytime TV talk shows. Nobody's going to break down and cry in here and there are no ugly, family screaming matches. Well, my brother did hit me because I stole his jazz drive while I was writing the book but that was just some latent childhood stuff coming out.

What I'm saying is, it's okay to have fun with the book. These are serious times, so I realize some of you feel you need special permission to have fun. But be advised that while you're laughing, I do expect you to be paying attention. Because I'm not playing with you here, boys and girls. All this stuff is true (well, most of it . . . a lot of it . . . some of it).

Don't let the fact that I graduated from the Barbizon School of Modeling throw you off either. Although I look like a model, I have substance. And by the way, it was between me and that model—that Tyson guy—for those Polo ads. I didn't get it because my butt was too high.

But, hey, I'm not writing this book to hold myself up as a role model. I just feel it is my burden here to share some of life's lessons with you. Plus I called the psychic hotline and she told me I would write a book. I wanted her to be right because I spent almost $100.

What makes me so qualified to share my guide to life? Well, let's see now . . .

- I dropped out of college.
- I was booted out of the Air Force.
- I'm divorced.
- I've been broke most of my life (even before I was divorced).
- I've been fired from every single job I've ever held

except as a comic, where I've managed to make a name for myself. I know, I haven't yet made a *last* name for myself, but I've made a *lasting* name out of the one I've got. Of course, now that I think of it, by today's key measuring standards of comedy stardom . . .

- I've got no TV series (and the only one I did have barely made it through one season).
- I am not in recovery (but I do know where the Betty Ford Clinic is).
- I am not dating someone half my age, of either sex (yet).
- I never did time (that anyone knows about).
- I work clean—no swearing, or sexy-clothes-wearing (because I can't fit into those tight pants).
- I've never been naked in a hot tub (at least there's no pictures of it).
- I've never killed an alien in a movie—though I did annoy Arnold Schwarzenegger a lot.

I know you're thinking, what do I have to teach you? After all, most of those self-help books are written by people who are members of Mensa. I could have joined but I didn't have the application fee. It's not just about being smart—it's about having a valid credit card. Do you want a book by one of those Mensa dudes or dudettes whose life has been one big breeze or by somebody like me who's been riding the *twisters* life throws at most of us?

Let's say you want to know about money. Do you think anything some billionaire will tell you in a book is going to help *your* situation, unless he tells you which dark street he walks down so you can jack him up? No, you want to hear from somebody like me whose checks have had some *mighty* bounces—I'm talking Michael Jordan verticals—but who still survived and never got arrested.

If you want tips on how to lead a dull, stable life and wear the right clothes for success, you can look somewhere else. Me, I believe you'll learn more worthwhile lessons from the man who couldn't hang on to a job, a woman, or a residence for any decent length of time ever. Someone who went from goofy kid to brain-damaged adult and is still smiling. Someone who's had his electricity turned off many times but has never been in the dark for long.

But, don't be looking for these pages to be a celebrity tell-all. I promised myself I wouldn't turn this book into a name-dropping, hair-salon-level gossip fest, spilling all the dirt I've got on my Hollywood, music, and sports star friends. (I also knew Shirley MacLaine in a past life—she was a black runaway slave and I helped her north to freedom.)

That's all in my next book. I'm holding out for the big bucks for that one. Then I'm telling everything.

Besides, I don't want to bore you with all those stories about me jamming with the Beatles (it was me who first told Yoko to just *shut up*); about teaching Dennis Rodman that rebounding is not enough—the hair is the thing; about how I sucker-punched George Foreman (he still doesn't know it was me); about my dives with Jacques Cousteau (he says the shark is our friend, but I saw one tear his butt up one time—he's still paying me not to release that footage of the shark that was *not* his friend); and teaching Baryshnikov how to pull the tights out of his butt without the audience noticing (tricky move!)—just to tease you with a few of my random memories.

And, of course, there is the now-famous story of my short time with The Jackson Five Plus One. That's right, The Jackson Five *Plus One*. They had an extra microphone and needed a guy to stand in front of it. I was that guy. You don't see me in the photos because cassettes were getting popular—and they were afraid there wouldn't be enough room for me on the cover.

I told them, "Look, let me show you boys a few steps and a few harmonies." But I didn't like it because that chimp was always making the floor wet (which is how Michael learned to moonwalk so slick), and I was the first to outgrow the clothes and the old man was too cheap to spring for a larger size for me, so I left. Not before Michael stole that whole Band-Aid on the fingers, high-pitched squeal number from me, which was how I always reacted to a paper cut in those days, "EEEEK!!"

But those are all the celebrity stories you're going to pull out of me. Especially don't go looking for *any* of my stories about Whitney or Barbra or Tom Cruise, because my lips have been sealed, but I won't tell you on *whose* Hollywood lips my lips have been sealed. Not now anyway.

Because I'm too young to be writing my memoirs yet. I've just turned forty, and yes, I have to admit even this finely tuned machine is beginning to slow down and swell up a little bit. If you take away nothing else from this book, let me give you one bit of important truth from the north side of forty: By the time you hit forty, you don't have any toes left. The end of your foot becomes one big corn with a toenail at the end. See that—even if you stop reading this book right now you've learned one big lesson that I wish I'd known when I was thirty-five. You've already gotten your money's worth from this book!

But, please don't stop. Because I, Sinbad, am an honest-to-goodness son of a preacher man. That's right, my father was a real preacher in Michigan, where our family grew up. (That means that my father won't lie, but I might.) So slide right into the book and be prepared to learn everything about anything. Also know that you are helping my children stay off the streets and go to college. The future of young minds—it's up to you.

Let Your Sinbad Self Sail!

People are always coming up to me and saying, "Sinbad, you're so *crazy*, man. How do you do it?"

I don't know how. There's a crazy gene that runs through my family that I must have been blessed with —mine is just more active than most. So, whatever you do, don't try to be me. I am *a professional* crazy person.

Let me put this rumor to rest: Even though Denzel and I look alike, we are not brothers, contrary to public opinion. I do wish we shared the same bank account. That's a joke, Denzel—I would never rob you. Not in daylight . . .

And now for the big questions: "What's your real name?" and "Why Sinbad?" I'm only going to answer these one time, so memorize it—don't ask me again out on the street.

You see, I always loved the character Sinbad, from

the first time I saw him as a small kid back in Michigan on our old black-and-white television when they would run the old Douglas Fairbanks, Jr., movies after school. Sinbad was the greatest sailor of them all, greater than Jason—not the maniac from the *Friday the 13th* movies, the Greek dude who fought all the monsters like Medusa, who had the biggest, nastiest weave in history, made out of snakes.

I was so fascinated by Sinbad the Sailor that I scoured the library looking for any information I could find about him. It was there that I discovered that Sinbad originally appeared in *The Thousand and One Nights*, not exactly the reading of choice for little brothers in sixties Michigan. But I sat in that library, hour after hour, all by my goofy, gawky self trying to break down his adventures into words that I would understand.

Sinbad made seven voyages back more than a thousand years ago, and he didn't know it, but I was his Afro'd companion for every one. Man, without a motor, that man could do some sightseeing! He was always searching for all kinds of treasures, which was fun to dream about. But what made my eyes bulge out were all the dangers he managed to crash into with his ships. Sure, there were shipwrecks, storms, and natural disasters, but my main man was like the coolest trouble magnet ever for the really strange stuff. Together him and me fought off whales as big as islands, huge, rock-throwing birds, and giant, hungry cannibals. And that could be in just one afternoon before I went to shoot some hoops.

I respected this Sinbad cat. He wasn't the biggest cat going and other guys had more muscles, but he seemed always to end up saving the butts of the bigger, brawnier men. He was a natural leader and kind of sneaky-clever. Whenever danger was breathing down his neck, when the roof was caving in, the ship about to sink, or every chip was down, you could count on Sinbad to save the day. He hung with kings, but he was most comfortable with the monsters, pirates, and thieves. I'm convinced that even though he spent his days on the seas, he would have been a major player or a mogul on today's streets.

I really liked the part of his legend that showed no one city, one adventure, or one woman could possess him. And I related to that part of Sinbad's personality that kept him from staying in one port for very long. He was a wanderer. He was a restless searcher. He thrived on adventure and didn't fear the unknown and there was no *known* thing that frightened him—or at least he didn't tell anybody. Who knows—what if there had been talk shows back then? He might have gone on TV and we'd have seen that he was scared of water, scared of women, and scared of monsters.

Over the years, since I've adopted the name as my own, and with it as much of his character and strength as I can muster, just saying "Sinbad" to myself when I'm feeling down has snapped me right out of my deepest funks.

"I'm Sinbad," I remind myself. "Sinbad doesn't give up. Sinbad goes the distance." There's nothing better that I can wish you than that you, too, will occasionally let your Sinbad self sail into adventures you've only dreamed of.

And by the way, my real name is . . . Dang, I ran out of ink.

I'm No Hero

Now you know the secret of my name, which I like to think inspires in me a certain fearlessness and a willingness to believe in the impossible. But I'm not going to lie: Believing in the impossible has a down side. It's one thing to have courage in everyday life—with the lights on—but when it comes to stuff like monsters, I'm gone.

I'm just a big scaredy-cat when it's dark in the house and there's a tapping on the window or a noise under the bed—don't even ask me to check it out. *You* go see while I hide out. I'm not a total coward; I mean, I love scary movies. Even when I was a little kid, I watched them: movies like *The House on Haunted Hill*, *Ten Little Indians*, *Thirteen Ghosts*. But then around the 1970s, the goriness came in: *Last House on the Left*—I'm talking bloody! Scare me, okay, but don't make me watch the ax come down and the arm get chopped off and the blood come squirting out. I beg you, please don't bleed all over me!

And how'd you like *The Exorcist*? That movie changed my life. I was standing waiting in that long, long line when Andrew, my friend from the basketball team, came out of the movie looking *whipped*. He was actually shaking. Andrew was pretty tough, so when he told me, "Don't go in there!" I should have listened— but no, I was too cool for that. So two hours later I was creeping to the car with my jacket pulled up over my head. I could hardly drive home, checking for Linda Blair to pop up in my rearview mirror. So right then and there, I invented a new ghost rule especially for the car: No ghost can get you with the dome light on. Yes, I was seventeen, but hey—that's a rule that helps protect me even now.

My original ghost rule was for bedtime: No ghost can get you if you are covered with blankets, but should any part of your body become exposed—look out! That's why I'd sleep with my head under the covers but during the night my dad would come in and pull them down. I would wake up sweating, freaking out: "Dad, don't you know you could have got me *killed*?"

I'm getting a patent on my special technique for watching scary movies, but I'll share it with you here. It's called *SQB*, the *Sinbad Quick Blink*. When the music gets loud and you know something scary's about to happen, you blink your eyes as fast as you can—like a strobe light in reverse—so when the head's chopped off there's a better than 50 percent chance your eyelids will be shut—but nobody ever has to know that you were scared.

You know what I hate: When some director tries to get cute and skip the scary music buildup to go straight to *bam!* bullet in the eye, snakes jumping out of the dead folks like in the Indiana Jones movies. Forget it, man, there's no way you can beat that! Maybe you could go to the director's house to jack him up— scare the living daylights out of him and ask: "How does that feel, huh? How do you think we like it? *Next time, don't leave out the scary music!*"

The one character in scary movies that I never understood is the vampire hunter. Why would anyone want to hunt down a vampire, especially when the vampire is not messing with *you*? I'm not *hunting* anything, that vampire is going to have to work for it, he's going to have to swoop down and find *me*.

In these movies, people always get bitten in the neck. To me, that means they don't even try to run. I'm telling you, if a vampire gets close to me, I'm off and running *away*! When they find my body, the police will scratch their heads and say, "Call in the *X-Files*, I've never seen this before. This man has two holes in his butt, and no blood in his body."

What are you going to do when you find the vampire anyway? And *why* do they always go looking for the vampire fifteen minutes before the sun goes down? They sit around talking about how they are going to kill him all day long, then wait until the sun is going down so they can make that mad dash for the castle to put the stake through his heart. If *I* was going to hunt a vampire, I would get a good night's sleep and start looking for him around 8 A.M., giving me plenty of time to look around the place for him. I would quit around 4 P.M. so I would have time to leave the city when I did not find him.

Lots of guys brag they'd fight off anything to save their woman. Yeah, right—you've got Count Dracula flying after you trying to suck you dry, and you've got your lady running behind you slowing you down. I don't know about you, but I would have to leave her. There is no sense in both of us dying. Someone has to live and tell the people what happened. I know what some of you ladies are thinking, "This is the nineties and we might outrun you." I agree, there are some fast sisters out there today. In that case I would just have to trip you then. You heard me, I would trip you.

Look, I would defend my woman against something small like a dog or even a regular crazy person, but not a vampire or werewolf. We're talking rip-your-throat-out-and-make-you-walk-the-earth-for-the-rest-of-your-life kind of guys. No woman is worth that kind of pain, not even Toni Braxton wearing one of those almost na-ked dresses (sorry, Toni). It's good-bye and good luck. The race is to the swift.

So the advice I would give to you people is to always be ready for the vampire. You never know when he might be in your town. Stay in shape, wear comfortable shoes so you can boogie or book up (means to run fast), and don't go out with strangers after dark. And if you are dating someone who is never around during the day, get the heck out of Dodge.

Smart as a Whip

Folks have asked me, "Does the fact that your father is a minister keep you spiritually grounded?"

Yes, that plus the fact that he still uses *the belt*.

Parents now let their kids get away with too much. Kids today holler at their parents, go off on their parents, and their parents go, "I don't know what to do." You know what to do. You've just got to do it. We've got too many books out now that tell you not to spank your children, it teaches them to hit others.

No, it doesn't—it teaches them to sit down and be quiet.

Just because you have kids doesn't make you a *parent*. You've got to step up to it and actually try to raise your kids. In the Midwest in the seventies, our parents certainly believed that. I don't know if it is realistic to expect it to take a village to raise a child, but I do know that back then anybody could whup a kid. You could get whupped by the whole neighborhood before you ever got home. People would be waiting and would rip off their belts as you walked by and start chasing you down the block, "I heard what you did!" Your butt would be swollen by the time you got home.

The weird thing is, some kids actually *liked* getting hit back then. I'd have friends come to my house and act wild so my parents would whup them. That's right —kids came to my house for whuppings. I didn't get it. I thought it was so cool that their parents left them alone. To me, that was *freedom*. But these kids told me, "You're lucky." Their folks weren't there or didn't care. They were hurting for discipline.

There were rules about whupping that every child knew. Number One: If you've got to get whupped, your father is the man. Mothers only whup you when they've lost their minds, and they don't stop until you're bleeding to death. All the while they're calling on God to stop their hand, as if they're possessed, and they're crying more than you are.

I only went off on my mama one time. I was ten years old. It was a Saturday, lawn-cutting day, and my father had left town for the weekend. My mother said, "Now, remember, your father said, 'Cut the grass.' "

"Well, he's not here, is he?" I don't know what happened, why those words came out. It was like some manly thing deep inside me, a voice that was saying, "Try it, try it. You're almost as tall as she is, she can't do anything to you."

If I had known then what I know now, I would have just tried to walk out of the room. No, I would have tried to *back out* of the room. For I heard a sound come out of my mama that I had never heard come out of her —and scarier than I had ever heard from anybody else.

"LORD JESUS CHRIST PLEASE DO NOT LET ME KILL THIS CHILD!"

There was echo and thunder and fire in that booming voice. I turned around and my mother was *growing*! Suddenly she was 6'10", with a suit on that had a *W* on her chest that stood for *whupping* and a big cape that was blowing in the wind behind her. Then a golden belt came out of the sky. She reached for it, gave it one mighty test lash in the air, and then in the voice again she yelled, "BY THE POWER OF SHE-RA I WILL KICK YOUR LITTLE BUTT!"

She hit me only one time and my butt fell off. Fell off on the floor. I picked my butt up and ran through the screen door and kept on running through the streets holding my butt in my hand.

Your mom can't outrun you, so I thought I was safe. But I forgot that God gave her that rubber extension hand for emergencies. "DON'T YOU RUUUUUUUUUUN FROM ME!" She snatched me back from eight blocks away.

My friends saw that hand coming, "It's your mama's hand coming. Just run—drop your butt and run!"

My mama got started whupping me and started praying at the same time. "JESUS, STOP ME NOW, LORD! STOP ME!!"

Now *I* started praying, "Lord, she's not playing."

I passed out. When I woke up it was Monday. I had missed the whole weekend. Mama came into my room. "Why did you make me hurt you like that?"

Oh, like I had begged to be whupped!

"You know I only whupped you because I love you."

"If it makes you whup me, then I sure wish you didn't love me that much!"

Now, fathers would just whup you until you passed out and then they'd quit—it was no fun for them once you were out. Early on, I learned what to say: "Oh, Daddy, you whupped me silly. I was unconscious there for a minute!" Sometimes, if there was time, I would add extra effect by putting an Alka-Seltzer tablet in my mouth before the beating so that when I crunched down on it I looked like I was foaming at the mouth. That always made a father feel good, like it was a job well done.

Rule Number Two: Never grab the belt, no matter how much the beating hurts. Resist that reflex action. The penalty in Michigan was twenty extra minutes of whupping—there was a clause about it in the state constitution, I think—even if you grabbed it accidentally, to save your life. Even if your hand said, "I can't let you take this no more! I got to save you right now," and for a split second you lost your mind. You're telling your hand, "Fool, let go of the belt!"

The belt is like the silencer on a gun. You'll have a bunch of kids in a room, acting up, screaming, "MINE! GIMME! HEY, THAT'S MINE!"

The father will go, "All of you quiet down!"

It has no effect. "MINE! GIMME! I'LL BITE YOU!"

"All of you go to your room!"

Still no response from those kids. "MINE! MINE! MINE!"

The father reaches to unbuckle his belt . . .

"MINE! MINE! MINE!"

The father is now holding the buckle and with one

continuous, dramatic sweep of his arm begins to pull off his belt . . .

"MINE! MINE! MI— Hey, everybody shut up! Dad's trying to talk to us. What do you want us to do, Father?"

The belt works.

Sometimes my father and I would play a little psychological game, like he would pretend that he didn't want to whup me. "How many times have I got to tell you?"

Now, I'm thinking that I can talk him out of it if I just agree with him. "I know, I know, Daddy. You're right, you're so right . . ." and this is probably where I overplayed my hand, when I started smacking my own head, "I'm just not getting it through my thick skull, am I, Daddy?"

It was like I had reminded him why we were there because before he finished the next sentence—"I talk to you and I talk to you"—*crack!*

You would try to distract him by pretending that he had really hurt you when the belt buckle would hit your hand—your hand that you had moved down to try to deflect some of the blows from your butt. "Ow, ow, Daddy, you hit my hand with the buckle!"

"Well, move your hand."

"Move my hand? I'm trying to save something down here!"

Then he would get annoyed. "Move your hand, I said!"

"Oh, that's so stupid. Just hit it. We've both got a job to do here, Dad. Your job is to hit me, my job is to stop you."

Talk to your children, the books today tell parents.

These books tell you to use a *time-out* with your kids. *Time-out?* You mean *chill time?*

You can just see a three-year-old sitting down, contemplating his wrong behavior, heaving a sigh, and getting up and telling you, "Why, you're right and I was wrong. Thank you for pointing out the error of my ways."

You know what's wrong with today's kids, why there's so much shooting today? The kids today have too much stuff. We didn't have anything worth killing anybody for in the seventies. Nobody wanted your raggedy jacket. You never saw anybody killed over a Kmart jacket. "Gimme your raggedy no-zip-it-up jacket!"

You'd say, "Here, take it. I was hoping somebody would get this jacket." You could take off the sorry jackets we had in the seventies, leave them on the ground, and even people who might be cold would walk around them, shaking their heads, saying, "I'm not wearing that raggedy thing."

Kids have everything now. Teenagers don't even know what they've got. They've got so much stuff they'll see things in their room, "Oh, I forgot about this."

We didn't forget about anything in the seventies. You knew where everything of yours was. "There's my three pairs of socks, there's my one *nice* shirt."

Teenagers today get to pick out their own clothes. They go to the mall and pick out $150 jeans for themselves. How you gonna buy some $150 jeans when you have no job? Your parents are making $400 a week and they're walking around practically naked because they can't afford to buy new clothes for themselves.

When I was a kid we usually weren't ever allowed to go shopping. We'd come home from school and our new clothes would be on the bed. You'd start stamping your feet and yelling, "Mama! I can't wear this *ugly* shirt! You can't make me wear that shirt. I'm thirteen!"

Mama would come running up the stairs. "Hey, Mr. Don't-Have-a-Job-Can't-Buy-Anything-for-Himself, you don't have to wear this shirt."

And she would take the clothes away from you, make you beg for that *ugly* shirt. I had to knock on my mother's bedroom door, "Um . . . Mama . . . could I have that shirt back? Mama, please, I know you can hear me."

"I thought it was an *ugly* shirt."

"I wish I could wear it today, that's what I was saying, Mama. I was just complaining how come I couldn't wear it *yet*."

That's how they would make you put those ugly clothes on.

When I was growing up you took your curfew seriously. As soon as the streetlight came on you better have your butt on your front porch. There was nothing to talk about, no negotiation.

One evening I mistimed it. I was outside and heard the call, "STREEETLIIIIGHT." I started thundering down my street. My father was already on the porch. "Boy!"

The light wasn't even up full, but I dove. *Boom.* All

the air was knocked out of me. "Wha . . . wha . . . what's for dinner, Dad?"

My dad was proud. "Look at how that boy *jumped*!"

The real challenge came when we were older, with the midnight curfew. There's no kid in the world who can make it home by midnight. You just can't. So when 11:55 came around, you had to make your choice.

"You going home?"

"No."

"You gonna take a beating. Me too, man."

You'd see each other at school the next day and you're all limping and sore. "I shoulda gone home. My daddy came home early."

Fathers liked it when you tried to sneak in, that's what got you in trouble. God protects parents by making everything in your path after midnight make some kind of noise. The sidewalk that is usually rock hard when you fall on it is going *squeak, crunch!! squeak, crunch!!* the second you put your party shoe on it. The birds up in the trees are going, "Tweet, tweet, SINBAD!!"

What really makes you look stupid is your parents hiding in the dark, waiting on you. Their eyes have already adjusted. Suddenly you're right on top of your dad. "What's up, Dad? I hope I didn't wake you up."

If you're going to take a beating don't take a 12:30 beating, take a *5:30* beating. You can only do this once, so make it a good party. Around five o'clock you'd get delirious with your friends, "Whoa, look at the sun come up! My daddy's gonna beat me. Wanna get something to eat? It's our last meal."

The situation didn't get real until you pulled up in front of your house and you tried your last shot, "Hey, you wanna come in? My mama will cook us some breakfast. Look, there she is in the window, waving at us."

"Yeah, something's gonna be smoking in there in a minute, but it sure won't be breakfast."

A *single* mother is worse than having a mother *and* a father. Usually, a mother can't stay up past eight. You come in and she's sitting in a chair. You hear this deep, deep voice that couldn't possibly be coming from your sweet mama. And the door isn't even locked, it's open a crack.

"COME ON IN, THE DOOR IS OPEN, MISTER PARTY-ALL-THE-TIME, MISTER PARTY-ALL-THE-TIME. MY SON WANTS TO PARTY ALL THE TIME, WELL, LET'S ALL PARTY TONIGHT." It's a scary scene.

M y father was kind of tricky sometimes. He'd catch me coming in late and, with my mother behind him, he'd start out kind of chuckling, "Heh-heh, you've just grown, haven't you, boy?"

"*Just grown,*" Mama echoes.

I go, "Mama, *sssh!!*"

"I say 'twelve o'clock,' you come in when you feel like it."

Followed by the Mama chorus, "*Come in when you feel like!*"

By this time my father's mad at her too for talking behind him and he's ready to hit everybody. I get the "*Hmmph!* You didn't know what time it was? *Hmmph!*"

It was that really dangerous *Hmmph!* when the lip tightens. That's the time you'd better answer with something.

"Nobody knew."

"Everybody with you and *nobody* knew?"

"No, nobody. Everybody was trying to figure it out and nobody had a watch and these people's house we were in didn't have electricity. If you had bought me that watch like I asked you for last year I could've come home on time. I thought it was eleven-thirty, because usually when it's dark like this it's *eleven-thirty* dark. You can call John. He thought it was eleven-thirty too."

"Hey, I'm not worried about your friends. Your friends jump off a cliff, you gonna jump off a cliff?"

"If I don't see the cliff." That makes him madder.

"Oh, so now I'm stupid. I see what your problem is. I'm just stupid to you, right?"

"No, Daddy, you are the most intelligent man I've known in my life. I know I don't have much life left right now, but up to this point, you the man."

My mother can't take it anymore, "BEAT HIM! BEAT HIM!"

Then she'd try to save my life. My mother would get me a worse beating and then she'd jump in and try to stop my father. "Oh, Lord, don't kill him! Lord, don't kill him!"

"Mama," I'd shout, "make up your mind!"

Then she'd come to me later. "Your father was just a little upset."

"Yeah, he wasn't that mad until you told him to beat me."

"Well, son, I was upset too."

• • •

The most imaginative whupping Daddy ever gave me came as a result of my crazy young interest in fires. Starting them.

I was alone one afternoon with my matches when I got the idea to see how close I could come with a flame to Mama's collection of poodles on the living-room knickknack shelf.

It wasn't much of an experiment. One match and the fake fur burned off all the heads of her poodles. I didn't panic. I just glued cotton to the poodles and replaced them on the shelf. They looked a little unusual, but as far as I was concerned, they were good as new.

But I wasn't finished yet. I checked over the room, hmm . . . the couch . . . the couch was a tempting object.

So, with a combination of fear and excitement, I struck a fireplace match, placed it dangerously close to the back of the couch, and watched the stuffing get sucked up by the flames. Science, man. It was over in a matter of seconds; the couch was intact, but its insides were gone.

At this point this young scientist should have quit. But this young scientist thought he understood exactly what would and would not burn. The young scientist was dangerously confident. The young scientist was an idiot.

The idiot was now in control. Or out of control. The idiot looked around the living room and considered Mom's prize possessions—her chiffon curtains. The curtains faced the sidewalk to show off Mama's beautiful taste. Chiffon, chiffon, thought the scientific idiot, is a fascinating combination of silk and rayon. But the young demented genius was having a good fire day, why not put a very small flame to the chiffon curtains just to see what would happen?

Puff!

Just like that, one match, one spark, and suddenly Mom's chiffon curtains were a burned-out mess of holes.

In those horrible few seconds, the scientist became a devout Christian, closing his eyes and praying, "Dear God, let me open my eyes and see that the curtains really aren't burned, and everything is just the way it was, and it's all a bad dream." He opened his eyes to the curtains, still pathetically burned. "Okay, God," said the former Christian, "if that's how you're going to play, I don't know how much longer I can worship you and keep calling you great."

The hour it took Mom to return home seemed like a hundred years. Naturally I closed the liners over the burned curtains, hoping she wouldn't notice them. I was hoping she wouldn't notice anything. Hoping against hope. Spraying so much wood-pine-scented Glade in the air that I was choking on the stuff.

The car drove up. Mom got out. Mom entered the living room. I was in the kitchen, reading my Bible lesson. I had returned to Christianity.

"Why is it so dark in here?" asked Mom. "Who closed the curtain liners?"

I ran into the living room to explain, "Mama, I didn't want that bright afternoon light to bother your eyes."

"Never heard that one before," Mom stated.

I wanted to give her all the love and affection a mother deserves. I was still praying she wouldn't notice a thing. But suddenly—and I swear it took the woman no more than twenty seconds—she had scoped out the room and was moving into all the red zones at once.

She was also sniffing. "Do I smell smoke? Why does my living room smell of smoke?"

I decided to sue the Glade company, sue them because their product is defective. And if their product is defective, other children, interested in other various experiments, may never have the chance to grow up and develop because they will be caught by their parents, and they will be maimed or murdered. I considered the distinct possibility that my parents might murder me.

My mother was inspecting her prized poodles. "Dear God," she said, "what is wrong with these dogs?"

"The dogs are outside," I said, referring to our real dogs.

"*These* dogs, son," she said, inspecting the cotton glued to their scalps. The cotton came off in her hand. Her poodles were BALD!

She put down the poodles and approached the closed curtains. She was smelling burned curtain. She was reaching for the cord that pulls open the lining. She was pulling the cord. She was looking at her curtains, pathetically burned. She was screaming at me louder than she had ever screamed before. I went running out of the house.

I was hiding under someone's porch. But by dinnertime, I was hungry, and I knew I had to go back. I arrived just before Dad. When he came in, right away Mom ushered him into the kitchen for one of those mumbling conferences where parents whisper low and kids try to understand what they're saying but can't. This time, though, the conference went on for less than thirty seconds when I heard Dad shout, "He WHAT!"

In a flash Dad was in the living room. Naturally I lied and said I had nothing to do with those fires. Naturally Dad ignored my lies. He was whipping off his belt and putting it on the floor. He told me to put all ten toes on the belt while he went upstairs for *another* belt. This was something new, but I knew it was not good. Now he was back downstairs. "Open the curtains," he said. I opened the burned curtains. He wanted this to be a public beating. "Now, hand me that box of fireplace matches," he said. "If you remove your toes from the belt, I'm starting all over again. Now, you light each of these fireplace matches, and as long as they burn, that's as long as you're getting whupped."

I always thought fireplace matches burned so fast. But I never knew any matches to burn slower. At one point I threw a match at Dad, hoping he might go up like the curtains. But the match never reached him.

M y brothers and I used to devise escape routes from my father. We used to get together like an army. "Okay, when he's chasing you, you'll see he's too big, just go down the steps and he'll bounce off the walls and you just slide down. Go through the kitchen—that little wall there will take him out." We never thought we'd need these escape routes, but one time my father was really mad. "This is it, this is the last beating! Come here!"

"No! You want to beat me, you come over here! Wear yourself out some before you get here."

My dad took off after me, and adrenaline took over my body. I saw my short life go before my eyes. I jumped onto the steps and I heard my dad stop short. *Bang!* I said to myself, "Wow, he did hit that short wall . . . It did work."

There was no time to admire my strategy. I was seeking my safest exit when I heard a groan that sounded like Dad coming from the kitchen. "He's *messing* with me," I thought. "He's trying to fool me. He can't be hurt." After a while I went back and my dad was lying on the floor with a knot on his forehead that was throbbing up, down, up, down, and turning ugly. Now I knew he wasn't playing. "Oh! Oh! He's dead!"

My mother came down and figured it out. "Boy, pack up your stuff. Don't come back. Wait until you're seventeen and lift some weights so you can fight back. Don't come back until then because when he gets up from there he's going to kill you where you stand."

I have a little brother named Mark who's my manager right now, and I used to mess him up just because he was younger and I could. Younger brothers can't protect themselves so you blame stuff on them and they take the beating.

When he was really little all he could do was look at me with a sad look that said, "Why are you always getting me in trouble?"

"Because you can't talk. When you can talk, then I'll blame it on somebody else. I'm not going to lie to you, it's going to be rough on you for a while. But I've been where you're at, and I survived it. By the way, we had another brother who died and we don't know where he is. Dad just beat him and put him in the backyard somewhere."

One of the dumbest things that parents do is to let you watch your younger brothers and sisters when you're twelve. My mother and father were like, "Now, your brother is going to watch you."

"No, please, Dad, please."

I would be like, "Don't worry. They'll be okay." My brother would hang on to the bumper of the car. "Don't leave, please!" He'd drop off the bumper once the car got up to speed and walk back toward the house and I'd be looking out the window.

"Come on and get your beating now, Mr. Tell-Everything. Come on and get your beating *now*. It's *payback* time."

In most of our homes, kids weren't allowed to go into the living room. You'd tiptoe to the edge and whisper, "One day, I'm gonna go in there! I'll be grown then and I'm even gonna sit down. One day."

When we were left on our own, the temptation to play on the perimeter was irresistible. On this day I broke one of my mother's favorite lamps playing basketball. I should have just quit playing. I should have never started.

"God, if you love me, you'll make the lamp just jump back up because I know you can do all things and you know my father better than I do, and if that lamp *doesn't* jump back, I'm dead."

I could have told my father that I broke the lamp, and he would have whupped me and then maybe he could have fixed it. But I decided I wasn't gonna take the beating. I took that lamp and pushed it back together and put it back on the table. Then I called out, "Hey, Mark, turn the light on."

Smash!!

"Oooh, look what you did!" It was cold-blooded, but it was funny.

Mark stood there crying, "I just touched it."

"I don't know what you did, I just know you broke it."

My dad didn't even get out of the car before I ran out yelling, "Daddy! Mark broke Mom's favorite lamp. I don't know what he was doing, he was playing with it or something."

Mark was standing there. "I did not!"

My father said, "You've done it this time! What were you doing playing in that room?"

"He told me to turn on the light!"

Hee-hee-hee! It's good to be the older brother.

The belt was mighty effective for keeping us in line, but leave it to my father to come up with a punishment that was even simpler and even more effective. It happened after the time I borrowed my father's car. All right, I *stole* it.

I was invited to a party that I really wanted to go to. My dad said I couldn't go. After he went up to bed I went anyway and I decided I might as well go in style, so I took his car, too. There I was, going to a party he had forbidden me to go to in a car—*his car*, the car I was forbidden to drive. I figured I would bring it home well before he woke up and ever realized it was gone.

I got to the party fine. The party was cool that night, the eight-tracks were smoking, but of course I didn't have any luck with any of the girls. Around midnight I slipped out and got behind the wheel of Dad's car. I turned the key in the ignition—you guessed it. Dead.

Dead car. Dead me. I prayed, "God, I know you're a mighty God who's moved mountains, so starting a puny little car engine isn't even a challenge. I wish I could give you a bigger challenge, but this is all I've got for now. So, please, let me put this key in the ignition here, let it start, and then let me start on my new life devoted to your service. If not, you may be seeing me a whole lot sooner than you want to—definitely a whole lot sooner than *I* want to."

My prayers were unanswered. My forehead was bathed in sweat, *fear* sweat. So I did the only rational thing left: I prayed to the devil. My thinking was, whoever got me home could have my sorry soul. I was turning my life over to whoever turned over the engine. After about a half hour praying to every divine power I could think up, I figured it was time to face my real maker. I called Dad.

His voice was filled with sleep. "You downstairs?" he asked. "You calling from another part of the house?"

I gulped hard. "No, sir."

"Where you calling from then, son?"

"Billy's house."

"No, that's not possible. *My* son's not at Billy's house. Billy's having a party and *my* son was told he couldn't go."

"It's about the car."

"The *car?*"

"The car."

"*Whose* car?"

I mumbled and slurred so my words were barely audible. "Your car."

"My car?"

"Yes, sir."

"*My* son was told not to take my car."

"Well, your son can't start your car. Your car's dead."

"Who's dead?" asked Dad. Before I could answer again, he said, "Just stay where you are. Wait for me *inside* the party."

I hated that part. It's bad enough to have my dad come rescue me, bad enough to think about the beating he was gonna give me, but to have it all happen in front of my friends was too humiliating to stand. "I'll wait outside, Dad."

"No, you won't," Dad insisted. "I'm coming inside to get you."

His words were nails scraping across my coffin. I stayed on the phone after he hung up and kept talking in case my party friends might be listening. "Yeah, okay, Dad. I love you too. Yeah, I'm just glad I'm not hurt, too. Yes, I'll wait here. Come on inside, we'll all be inside. Bye-bye."

The minute he showed up in the doorway of the party the eight-track stopped dead in all eight tracks. Songs we'd been listening to like "Oh, What a Night" and "Didn't I (Blow Your Mind This Time)" suddenly took on new meaning.

Dad looked straight at me. "Let's go, son," he ordered, leading me out like I was a little boy. I felt two inches tall.

When we reached the car, I told him, "I tried, believe me, it's not going to start."

Paying me no mind, he lifted the hood, fished a flashlight and tool from his back pocket, and tinkered for about ten seconds. Back in the car, behind the wheel, he turned the key and the engine hummed like it was showroom new.

Driving home, the silence was thunderous. Just before we got to the house, I heard him say, so faintly that I had to strain to hear, "The thing that hurts me most is that my son would lie to me."

He didn't raise a hand. He didn't say another word.

The next morning I was up at seven, cooking him breakfast, buttering his toast, asking whether he'd rather me mop the floor or paint the house. But Dad just looked at me and shook his head. "Boy," he said, "that lie really hurt me."

By day's end, I was thinking, "Go ahead and beat me, Dad. Anything's better than this feeling that I let you down."

After that, Dad owned me for about two years.

Money: Too Tight to Mention

Can you pay for it? That's the number one question. Get a job, fall in love, buy a house, buy a car; it's the same—you got what it takes? And if you don't, you end up the same—jacked up; call it any name you want: fired, divorced, evicted, repossessed.

And how are you gonna pay? Cash, credit, layaway? Layaway I've hated since I was small. Go to the store, pick out the cool pair of pants, know you're looking good. Then you go to pay, and Mama's messed you up: "Here's ten dollars down, and we'll put a dollar in a week."

A dollar a week? It can take a whole life to pay off that layaway. You visit your clothes and watch them go out of style. Then, fifty-five years old—"I'm picking up the burgundy sharkskin pants, boys' size six."

Layaway tickets handed down for generations! Folks

even leave a layaway ticket in the will, like it's some kind of family heirloom. Like I'm actually going to Kmart with the layaway ticket to pick up that pair of slippery-sliders, the kind of shoes get you killed playing dodge ball.

Still, layaway clothes were a luxury in my family. Six kids—my mama would sew, and those clothes were made to last. Two suits in one: powder blue on the outside; and when it got dirty, inside there was purple plaid. No zipper—just a strip of Velcro to get old and fuzzy and then you'd stand up in class and your pants would pop open. Girls laughing: "Ooh, he's wearing Spiderman underpants." I was eighteen years old at the time . . .

I'm a father now, so I know kids' feet grow at least an inch a day, and I can understand how hard my parents worked to keep us in shoes. But as a child I used to dread our trips to Kmart—the six of us crowding the bargain table, where all the shoes were tied together on one long string. Like, "Don't let them get loose or they'll stampede." Mama would tell us, "Now, this time, only two of y'all are getting shoes." And I'd pray, "Please, not me!" Those shoes were too tough to bend or crease; they'd defend your feet like steel or wooden shields. You could walk through fire in them and never feel a thing, but you'd be walking like Frankenstein—that's how tight they squeezed.

Tight as they were, they couldn't hold on to our tube socks, the kind that cost a dollar for a hundred pair. Soon as you pulled them up, the elastic in those socks would explode, so they'd roll off your feet and jump right out of the shoe! Remember all those socks you'd see on the curb when we were kids? They'd all jumped off people's feet and got washed down to the gutter when it rained.

At least those cheap clothes and shoes and socks were new, not just "new to you" like a lot of our stuff. In the Midwest when I was growing up, rummage sales were the key to life. In California—drive up in the Mercedes-Benz, play like they're looking for antiques —folks like to call them "estate sales." Who are they trying to fool? If there's a piece of cardboard nailed to the light pole, with an arrow pointing to your house, it's a rummage sale: You need some money, we need your old stuff.

My mother is Benton Harbor's Golden Gloves champion of the rummage sales. She's gentle and sweet, a preacher's wife, but she can take care of business. Some women train for rummage sales—weight lifting, kick boxing—but not my mama; after raising six kids, she thought gyms were for amateurs. I've seen her kung-fu fight for a cashmere coat—whup twenty women, get that coat to the table, then power-bargain, not even catching her breath. "Ten dollars! Why, this isn't worth five. I'll give you three . . . Not seven, three-fifty . . ."

The other women are all still gasping on the ground. I'd get so embarrassed that I'd pull out the dollar I'd made from cashing in bottles. "Here, Mama, please pay her four-fifty and let's leave."

"I'm not paying a penny more than three seventy-five . . ." She was tough.

And fast. The second she heard, "There's a better sale on Robin Street," she would haul butt, cutting down the alleys and switching back to ditch the competition. She was one of those queens of the rummage sales—when she showed up, you knew that your sale was a good one. Friday night was when the signs would get tacked to the telephone poles, and my mother would drive around trying to sniff them out. We'd be sitting in the back of the station wagon and we'd see that familiar piece of cardboard tacked to a pole, and we'd be praying: "Please, don't let Mama see it." But my mama wouldn't miss it. She had excellent rummage sale peripheral vision—she could see 180 degrees behind her without using the rearview mirror. *Screeeech* —she's stopped the car, she's backing up. "What does that say?"

"Mama, I can't read it, it's too dark out."

"You will read that sign . . ."

It got so on Saturdays other women would stake out our street, sitting there at dawn on our lawn with their motors idling, watching for my mother to make her move.

The worst thing was, she made us all go to the sales with her. Then you might as well say good-bye to your pride. Right in the backyard, she'd toss you some pants: "Here, try these on."

"Where?"

"Just take off your pants. Hurry up."

"Mama . . ."

"You've got nothing for anyone to see."

"Thanks, tell the world . . ."

I'm standing there in my rummage-sale Spiderman underwear, a station wagon pulls up—"Look at him!" —kids are laughing. And I know I can never go back to school again.

That taught me a lesson: to jump out while Mama was parking the car and get to the sale first. She was surprised, but I lied and told her I liked shopping. Mama, let me finally confess the truth, here and now: I was running around finding everything that would fit me so I could hide it from you.

The worst rummage sale item she ever got me was a pair of green Adidas. All I'd ever seen was white Adidas, so I thought they were supercool. She was proud too: "You don't find too many pairs of size thirteen shoes for fifty cents." But when I wore them to basketball practice, I kept smelling fumes and the green seemed to be cracking. Someone had spray-painted those shoes.

Then one of my teammates came up to me: "Hey, those are my shoes! Where'd you get them?"

"Uh, my mama found them someplace and wanted me to get them back to you."

"I don't want them. I threw them out."

"You did? Here they are anyway." And I walked home barefoot, my head hanging low.

My mother was a trashpicker too. She actually took an upholstery class in case she spotted some "antique" out on the curb, so she could take it home and fix it. In the eighties she upgraded to bungee cord, but when I was young we always carried clothesline with us in case something didn't fit, so we could tie the trunk shut or rope it to the top of the car. One time, she found a couch. "Let's just take it," I said, but no—she forced me to get out of the car and ring the doorbell. "Uh, hello, my mother wants to know if we can have that couch out of your trash . . ."

The woman thought we were so pitiful: "Oh, we're throwing out some tables and a chair too . . ."

"No! No! We just want the couch!"

Now I know what I should have done: Rung that bell and when the woman answered, said, "My mother thinks that couch in your trash is the ugliest thing she's ever seen. Get it off the street, or else we're calling the police."

My father had a different approach to thrift. He was the fixingest man you've ever seen. If Mama found something broken at a rummage sale, she'd reserve it for my daddy with her "swoop back" technique. Like a TV—in the morning, Mama would say she was interested just to get the man's hopes up, then all day he'd be expecting someone to meet his price. Right when the sale was closing, Mama would swoop back—"Oh, I see you've still got that old TV. Well, it's still not worth twenty dollars." By then the man would let her have it for five dollars rather than haul it back in the garage. And within a few days, my daddy would have it up and running, having spent only fifty dollars to fix it. Then we'd have to hear the story over and over again—on how he and only he could have saved that TV set.

One time my sister totaled the car; it hit a gas pump and blew up. But even though he got the insurance money, my father towed the car back home. He had to buy sheet metal, but he rebuilt that car—he just couldn't let it go to waste. Sometimes we resented his ability to fix things. I had a cool-looking bike—purple Sting Ray, with big handlebars and a yellow banana seat—but it was cheap. Every couple months, the handlebars popped off. Almost got me killed. But my father just kept welding those handlebars back on until the bike was nothing but one big gray weld—"Look out! Big lump of solder rolling down the street!" Folks would scream and jump out of the way. The only thing on it that still looked like a bike was the banana seat.

When my dad needed expensive tools for his projects, he'd watch for those ads: "Use it free for thirty days." He'd get the tools, build a porch on the house, and then send them back on the twenty-ninth day. The Number One and Number Two laws in my house were "Never throw away the box" and "Never throw away the tags." To this day my home is filled with boxes and tags for stuff I might have to take back—hey, you never know. And when I got to college, I followed my dad's example. I'd buy some disco clothes, wear them that night, and get my money back the next day. I couldn't dance—couldn't take the chance that I'd sweat in those clothes—but I looked cool.

I feel lucky that my parents were thrifty. Because of rummage sales and my dad's fix-it capability, I could wear cool clothes and have things that a family at our income level wouldn't usually have. Early on I learned to bargain and to fix things. And I must admit that every now and then I use the swoop-back technique to see if it still works. Those old habits die hard.

But, hey, it was tough asking thrifty parents for money. You've got to beg fathers: "Dad, can I have a dollar?"

"What happened to the dollar I gave you last year?" And then get the lecture: "Boy, let me tell you something. Money doesn't grow on trees . . ."

You have to act like, "Oh, man, I didn't know that,"

when what you want to say is, "If it did, I'd be outside picking it, not in here fighting with you."

Girls are better at getting money out of fathers; they get all conniving, sit on his lap—"You're just the smartest and handsomest daddy in the world." Don't even have to ask—he's writing a check.

Mothers will cry when you ask for money, but they'll always try to give it to you. "Mama, I need $500."

"Oh, child, here, take it, don't worry about us—we'll just bounce our check to the landlord. Pray we don't get evicted or go to jail . . ." You feel bad.

The best person to ask for money is your grandmother. Grandmothers always have money—no job, haven't worked in fifty years—it's like God puts magic money in their purses. "Grandma, I need $2,000."

"Let me just look in my pocketbook . . . Oh, here's $2,500. Buy yourself a treat . . ."

Growing up without money makes you strong, shows you another way to look at life. Like when my car got repossessed—the first of many times—it hurt me. But the next time the repo man snatched my car, I didn't cry. I looked on the bright side: "Now I have no more debt and I don't have to fix the eight-track. That repo will save me $400 a month. With all that money, I can get a new car. I can get a better one." And I was grateful. Thank you, repo man.

When you start making money, things change. Like credit cards—I still don't understand the concept. They encourage you to use them, then they want your money—and have the nerve to have an attitude about it. There's something about plastic that makes you get things you'd never buy for cash. With cash, you're careful: "You got one smaller and cheaper? A plastic one for $1.99? No, that's good enough. It doesn't have to be real, just look it." But when you're charging it, you want the best, the super-duper model for $50. "Give me that TV with the twenty-foot screen—I've got to have it. My family can go live in the garage."

Before computer technology, checks were a great thing. Local ones took fourteen days to clear; out of state, maybe six months. No money? Go on, write a check—then go out and get a job. But nowadays they love to embarrass you. You're in the checkout line, twenty people behind you, the girl goes to the phone.

"Who're you calling?"

"We have a new system, sir. We check your balance with the bank."

"What? Don't go calling them! Those folks at the bank don't know me."

"Oh, yes, they do. They're garnisheeing your wages for the IRS . . ." Whole store's laughing. "There's a lien on your house and you're overdrawn . . ."

Naturally, I have to put my attitude on: "I'm not shopping here! Put back all the stuff—y'all charge too much. I'll just pay cash for this banana."

Still, don't ask me to balance my checkbook. That's no job for a man. Man opens an account, writes down the amount, then uses the checkbook for a telephone book—names, addresses, numbers. Meet somebody fine, rip out a deposit slip and put your phone number on it, like it's a business card. Woman thinks, "Hmm, he's got a bank account—the man must have a job."

Maybe it's just me, but did you ever notice that when you go to the bank to cash a check—even if you've got the money to cover it—you feel guilty? It's like there's a conspiracy against you. When the teller says, "I'll be right back, sir," you start to sweat. Now he's talking to the branch manager and they both glance at you with that evil eye. You start to doubt yourself. Even if you've got a billion dollars in the bank, you start thinking, "Maybe it's not in there . . ." Then you know what to do: Like a coward, you turn tail and run out of the bank.

Or you can use those automatic cash machines instead. It used to be once you were broke in the mall or ran out of money gambling at the casino, you went home. But now they have these machines where you can stand in line to get cash so you can get broker and broker and broker. In the good old days you could fool those machines—put in a fake deposit slip, made out for $400, and the machine would give you back money like you had cash. Now they actually arrest you—the nerve of them!

And is it just me, or have you ever gone to the ATM machine knowing you've got no money in the bank— your account might even be closed—hoping to confuse the machine into giving you money? It has been known to happen!

Folks go crazy when there's someone with a new card holding up the line. *Beep, beep*—he stuck it in wrong; the machine spits it out. *Beep, beep*—his code won't work. Try again—*Beep, beep, beep* . . . everybody wants to jack up a guy like that. Anytime someone's holding up the line, try this technique: Get right up behind him: "Wow, you got a lot of money! You ought to loan me some." He'll learn fast. The whole line will cheer and maybe even lend you five or ten dollars. You'll be the hero of the mall.

• • •

Being broke teaches you that money can't buy happiness, though you will be happier if they don't cut off your phone and your utilities. I think there should be a law so they can't cut off all your stuff at one time. You should be given the chance to pick one or two out of the four—maybe the phone and the lights, or maybe the phone and the heat. One thing they should never be allowed to cut off is your cable TV. That is just cruel and unusual punishment!

So what else can I tell you about money? First of all, don't worry about balancing your checkbook—just keep writing checks until they start to bounce. The bank will let you know. It's their job. Besides, they charge a ten-dollar fee—bouncing checks is good for the bank, it's good for you, and it's good for the country! Any trouble, just do what the old ladies do: Throw a hissy fit. *"Do you know who I am?* I just put $20,000 from my income tax refund into this bank!" Always remember, it's only money—they print more every day.

Last but not least, never argue with the women at the phone bill window. They have no heart.

We're Not from Mars, We're from Down the Street

Ladies, quit having your discussion groups. We men are *not* from Mars. We are from here in the neighborhood, just down the street. We *are* different from you, nobody's arguing that. We are trouble, sometimes. Goofy, maybe. Lazy, not all of us. True, we will always do those dozens of big and little things that make you crazy—it's genetic—just like it must be genetic that you will always believe that you can—and must—*change* us.

If you check the Bible, of course, the trouble started right at the get-go. Adam was having a perfectly cool time by himself, running around naked, hanging with the animals. God said, "Whoa! I told him not to eat those apples and he's not eating the apples. I give him one rule, and he's sticking with it. How dull is this?"

Before you know it, God takes Adam's rib (of all the

body parts, why the rib, God?) and here comes Eve, and sure enough, first thing she does is start nagging Adam, "You call yourself a man? If you were a real man, you would eat the apple for me."

So right from the start what's he trying to do? Trying to please a woman.

"Oh-oh-oh-kay, Eve, honey, if you want me to."

Then *zap*!! They're busted. Immediately Adam blames all of his troubles on his woman. "God, she *made* me! I didn't even like the taste of the apple. Can I stay in the garden? Just leave me with the monkeys. Those monkeys were cool."

God sent them packing together. And then, begat after begat, from generation to generation, men just got stupider and stupider trying to please women.

Samson—the dude slays a thousand people, as long as he doesn't cut his hair. Delilah shows up and he starts thinking, "How bad could it be? I'll just get a little *fade*."

If there were no women in the world, men would be naked, driving trucks, living in dirt. Men never would have built big tall buildings just for themselves. Women came along and it gave us a reason to comb our hair, but that doesn't mean that we will be any more manageable for you than our hair is for that comb.

Remember, our mothers couldn't handle most of us men, so what chance do you have? Men are moody by nature. Most men are mad at their job, they're mad at their children, they're mad at the rich, the poor. A man always thinks somebody else has a better situation than he's got going on, like the single guy is jealous of the married man's stability at the same time that the single guy's freedom gnaws at the married man's gut.

Mind you, I'm not seeking any sympathy, sisters. Oh, I could see that *Oprah* show, "Today on *Oprah: Men Who Have Been Burned.* Watch men share and cry just like real live dolls." Women would organize drive-by shootings of the studio within five minutes. I don't think the national 800 number for men who need a spiritual hug from another man is going to have a lot of calls either: "Hello, caller, what's your name? Larry? Well, you are loved. Hello . . . Hello . . . Next caller, please!"

No, if men are to be saved, it's up to you women. At least that's what most of you think, despite centuries of evidence that when it comes to men, what you see is what you end up getting.

If a man is a jobless bum when you meet him, he'll be a jobless bum husband if you marry him.

Women see the miracle that *could* be—why else would convicted murderers in prison get love letters? Women would like to believe there's this proper little *neat* boy we are just keeping squelched down inside ourselves, a good little boy they can release with enough yelling and ammonia fumes. Nonsense. If you go over to your boyfriend's apartment and you can't see his floor because he's got all his clothes and junk lying around, and you move in with him anyway, you can bet it will now be *your* floor that you cannot find.

"I'm not here to pick up behind you," you shout in vain at his sloppy, hopeless hide.

"*Don't* pick it up," that's his response. "I didn't expect you to pick it up. Just leave it there, I'll find it next time I need it."

If you ask most women what they want from a man, without hesitating, most of them will turn into Aretha, belting out:

R-E-S-P-E-C-T

Yeah, sister. It's more like:

R-E-$-P-E-C-T

If a poor man respects you, that's nice, but if Mr. Moneybags tips his hat, that's love.

That's right, for if a man looks like he's got money, he could look like a dead baboon's butt and most women would go, "Mmm . . . I like a little *monkey* in my man." A man could have his ear half torn off and dangling down, if it's got a big diamond stud stuck in it, some woman will tell her friend, "That ear doesn't bother me. We're not going to do that much *talking* anyway."

You see it over and over. A man's driving along in his perfectly adequate Honda. He sees a woman waiting for the bus. *Beep-beep.* "You want a ride?"

"Not in *that*!"

"Well, it's better than those *Hush Puppies* you're pushing down the street."

But if a Rolls-Royce pulls up, she drops that attitude real fast, even if Freddy Krueger himself slithers out of the driver's seat. "Oooh, Freddy! Girl, he's kinda cute, with those big, long fingers. Freddy! Burn me up! I was dreaming about you last night, Freddy."

If he had the keys to a Porsche, the *Elephant Man*

could get a date. "That bag on his head is *sexy*. He's
got it going on. Just don't let him fall asleep."

The more money he has, the fatter and uglier a man
can be. Men, instead of going to the gym, get a good
job. If you've got enough *whip* out, you never have to
work out. It will save you a lot of time and sweat at the
gym. You see a lot of *bad* women with fat guys, but
they're not hanging with any *poor* fat guys.

And women are always going on about how they like
older men because they are so *wise*. "He has all that
wisdom in his eyes." Oh, yeah? I've never seen women
draping themselves all over a *poor* old codger. A homeless guy could be holding up his begging sign written
in perfect classical Latin, there's nobody going to pull
over to pick him up except maybe some little ol' nun.
No other woman is going to be thinking, "He looks so
distinguished pushing his cart down the street!"

Of course, men are even more shallow, but our focus
is a little different. For us, it's usually the *physical* that
gets us going. Not for us that old fairy tale about *inner
beauty*. It's a fact that if you left an ugly woman and a
gorgeous woman side by side along the road, both of
them with flat tires and no equipment, the ugly
woman's only hope is if she's got a really strong set of
lungs and can blow up that tire herself.

A fine woman could have killed nine or ten people,
all a man will say is, "She's not trying to kill me."

"Man, she's killed people!"

"As long as she's not killing *me* yet, she's all right.
All I know is she's fine. Besides, I'm not trying to
marry the woman."

●   ●   ●

Women have a bond that men don't understand. When you break up with one woman, all of her friends hate you. You are at a party and you start talking to a woman and she goes off on you, "Don't even try to talk to me, you *dog*. Tracy is my friend, and I heard what you did." You have to go on a road trip to get a date.

Now, women always say men are "dogs." Well, sisters, you can play the game just as hard as men, 'cause you can't have a dog without a "cat." Meow, baby, we're not dogging by ourselves.

A woman knows you're going out with her best friend, let's say, but she's one of those women who like the thrill of taking from another woman, so this gal will come slinking around you, "Mmm . . . honey, why you going out with her?"

"Well, you know, she's *cool*."

"Oh, that's too bad, because I sure like you, too."

Now you know that is too much pressure for one man (we needed that "borrowed" rib to handle the pressure). A man has to go for it or he'll just bust.

I'm telling you, women, be very careful when your friends try to give you advice about your man. It's like you don't want to have a bald beautician cut your hair because she'll get out those sheep clippers and shave you before you blink your eyes because she doesn't like the fact you got more hair than she does. "Girl, it's summertime, you need to cut all this off." If your girlfriend has nobody, she's not the one to listen to for help with your man. She may want him for herself. "Girl, you should let him go. He's *crazy*. I don't know why you stay with him." So, you break up with him and next thing you see is her out with him. "Oh, I know he's crazy. I'm crazy, too. That's why I like him. I was trying to save you, girl. I didn't want you to be hurt."

Generally, though, women support each other when the cause is being mad at you. When a woman really gets mad, she wants to show *everyone* that she's mad at you. The other women in the room will automatically get mad at their men too. It's like a chain reaction. They start hollering at their men, who aren't doing anything.

"See, that's what you do! All of you have the same problem!"

The man has to start apologizing for something he doesn't even know he did wrong.

"Baby, I was just asking you if you wanted a Coke."

Now your woman is mad because you had the nerve to not know what she is talking about.

"Oh, I'm crazy now!"

Women, when you are mad at us, please just *tell us* you're mad. Don't make us play the "Oh, Are You Mad?" game. See, we are not stupid, we know we did something wrong; we just don't know which one you found out about. How many times have you come home and your woman is slamming cabinets because she wants you to really *know* she is there. "Honey, is everything all right?"

"Yes." *Slam!!* "Fine." *Slam!!* "Can't I just shut some doors?"

Just back out the door you came in and keep going. Some fools will try to engage in conversation at this point, usually newlyweds. Bad move, bad move. About the only thing I think works is to quickly shout, "Okay, I'll be right back." That will temporarily confuse and distract her and then you can haul butt out of the house.

Some women will just lead us on with their anger to see how much we'll confess to, which is usually a lot, because men are such terrible liars. Women can tell when we are lying because we start stammering and stuttering and we put our heads down. You have to practice your lie so well that even you start believing it. Men, you know you are good when you get in an argument with your lady about something and you forget it was a lie. You actually get an attitude with your woman. It is not until later when you are by yourself that you remember, "Man, I forgot I was lying!" You have to train like a Shaolin priest, until the lie becomes real—only then will you be ready to leave the temple, Grasshopper.

Most importantly, men, when you lie, stay with the lie. Start writing down your lies if you have trouble keeping them all straight. Enter them in your laptop, your Wizards, or whatever digital device you use to store your information so you can carry your lies around with you. It might save your life one day.

Even if they have video footage and witnesses to challenge you—and believe me they will—you must stay strong. No matter what happens, *stand* by that lie, *embrace* it, *love* it, *lie down* with it. Keep saying, "That's my story and I'm sticking to it, unh-huh!" You might go down, but at least you will go down swinging. And that is what relationships are all about, being able to say, "I'm still here!"

Matching and Accessorizing

If there is a difference between men and women, it would have to be how they put different items together. Men don't have to match or have a matching set for something to be functional for them.

But a woman will not feel comfortable, for example, in a shower unless she approves of the shower *curtain.* And of course, the towels must come in sets. If the towel sets are split, say the hand towel is a crisp Autumn Harvest and the body towel's a Peach Blush—forget it. And heaven help us if the washcloths are a third shade, say a sassy Evening Rose—that woman would probably have to lie down for a week. Just put the orange washcloth with the green towel, woman! They'll dry you all the same. "Can you believe their towels didn't match!" She would rather stay funky than clash.

Most women believe that everybody has bad taste in fashion and decorating except for themselves. Of course, nobody has *worse* taste than their man. A woman you just met will come into your house and the first thing out of her mouth is, "You can tell a bachelor lives here."

I reply, "In case you hadn't noticed, I *am* a bachelor and I *do* live here." Then, without blinking an eye she'll tell you everything has to go—like you hired her to redecorate your house. All I wanted to do was take the girl to a movie.

It's the same when women pick over their outfits. They're always messing with the *ensemble*—that word "ensemble" irks me. Men don't have ensembles—we have pants and shirts and hopefully some socks that match. Why do women believe that every outfit has to have *accessories*? And a *choice* of accessories, to boot. "Honey, aren't you dressed yet, it's been two hours."

"Don't rush me, I'm *accessorizing*."

I believe all women should dress like New York women, just go the basic black route and wear the same four black outfits to death. That way everything will match, almost. They still have eighty-seven different pairs of black shoes. Ask her why and she says, "They are *not* all the same color. If you would just look you would see that they are different shades of black." Arrrrgggggg! For men, black is black—there are no shades of black, those are called *gray*.

We know that most of the time you're not dressing up for us—you're dressing to impress other women. Women never tire of analyzing what other women are wearing and about each other's body parts. "Ooh, girl, with your butt you can wear that. Try it on. Oooh, look at your butt. It's so cute. My butt's too big. I could never wear that."

You'll never hear two men going, "Oh, man, with your butt, those pants are *definitely* you!"

Men can't even say the word *underwear* when we're together. But just because we don't spend time talking about it doesn't mean that men don't have a special relationship with their underwear. Men don't buy underwear for the way it looks. In fact, for the most part, men don't buy underwear, period. It takes a man a good seven to nine years to really work-in a pair of underpants to the desired level of comfort. We're talking bleached-out, saggy, no-more-crotch, sagging-elastic underpants, with at most one Fruit of the Loom guy barely hanging on for dear life.

Most of the time, at the end of the day men will take off their underwear and throw it on the floor. You women should try this sometime. It's very liberating. Some men have a further ritual that is either more or less advanced, depending on your feelings about laundry and health code violations. This method is an outgrowth—"growth" being the key word—of their college years, when the trick was to postpone doing laundry until they graduated.

These guys will take off a pair of underpants and put it in the One Day pile in the drawer. That same pair, after the next wearing, will work its way in orderly fashion into the Two Day, then Three Day piles, and so on, until it finally gets up on its own and walks into your bathroom and takes a shower.

Generally, underwear is about the last thing a man thinks about. But your woman is always reading one of those stupid magazine articles about "How to Make Your Man Feel Like a Sex Machine All Day Long." And they always end up urging your woman to buy you some *bikini underpants*.

Women,

DO NOT BUY YOUR MEN
BIKINI UNDERPANTS!

You got a man whose gut is hanging down to his calves and you're buying him bikini underwear? Are you crazy? Have you ever looked at bikini underpants for men? They look like knee pads, which is about how your man will use them, because he'll never pull them up past his knees. And if he does get them all the way on, he may *start out* with those bikini underpants around his butt, but I guarantee, he'll never make it out of the bedroom without them ending up *inside* his butt. He'll take about two steps and *whoosh! there they go*, just sucked up inside his butt before he makes it out of the bedroom.

Now, you women take your underwear very seriously these days. I remember when I was a kid, every girl just wore the same big, plain white underwear. One day a girl came to school with blue underwear and we didn't know what to make of this. You are probably wondering how I knew her underwear was blue. I was the king of two very important junior high techniques, the mirror-on-your-shoe technique and the drop-your-pencil-and-look-up-the-girl's-dress-in-the-desk-behind-you technique.

Times sure have changed. Now you women spend a fortune at Victoria's Secret. Your underwear costs more than the clothes you've got on the outside.

Why? It's no secret to us, Victoria!

Men don't care that much about your underwear. Who told you that we did?

Once you start taking *off* clothes, we don't care if your underwear has holes in it, is mismatched, turned inside out, or you don't have any underwear on at all! Do you think we're going, "Oooh, that there is some nice underwear. No, keep it on for a while. Is that a matching set? Don't take it off—let me sit here and watch it for a while."

Of course, women feel they must wear matching underwear, and of course you will not mix and match. "I lost my red bra, I've got to get a whole new set." Why? Not for us—go ahead and wear the green bra with red underpants. We'll think Christmas came early.

Yes, y'all will always look for new ways to drive yourselves crazy about your underwear. I remember when women used to wear that one-piece bra and panty girdle outfit, *jumpsuit underwear,* that used to be in one piece that went up over the shoulder. Every once in a while, the rubber would just pop out of the middle and the woman would have to whisper, "Girl, I've got to go home. My panties just *exploded.*"

And now you've got some underwear that will really mess with a man's mind. The Wonder Bra. Just when a man is thinking, "Wow, she's really something!" the woman takes off her Wonder Bra and he's screaming, "NO!! NO!! YOU LIED!! PUT IT BACK ON!!"

Don't get me wrong, ladies, we do enjoy the little stripper routines you perform for us in your Victoria's Secret outfits. We just don't require as much as you do. Take strip clubs, for instance. The difference between how men and women approach those shows really cracks me up.

If a man wants to go to a strip show, he's got to lie. He's got to park, like, in Los Angeles, then walk back to a strip club in, say, San Jose and sneak through the back door of the building so he doesn't get caught. Ladies get to go to a room with decent lighting where the men are really *built*. Our clubs have two dim red lightbulbs and if a woman can breathe, they allow her to take her clothes off. I have actually seen men shout, "Put it back on!" If you saw what they give us, ladies, you would encourage us to go to those clubs.

Women, though, are right up front when they want to go to a strip club. "Give me a hundred dollars. In *ones*." Then they go and they lose their minds. They're all fighting to sit in the front row and they're screaming.

"Yeah, bring it here, boy!"

"Don't you run from me!"

"I got something for you—come and get it!"

Old women in wheelchairs will be popping wheelies trying to get closer.

Now, explain this to me. A man you don't know puts his butt in your face, a sweaty butt, a butt you don't know where it has been—and for that you give him money? And the closer his butt, the more he gets?

Okay, since this is what you like—men, try this at home tonight. When your woman is sitting down watching TV, pull your pants down and jump in her face. I bet you'll get a different reaction. "Get your butt outta my face!"

"Yeah, down at the strip club, you'd be pounding on the table."

"I don't want *your* butt in my face!"

"Can I get a dollar anyway?"

"All right, but you'll have to stuff it in yourself."

"It's a deal."

Dating: The Thrill of Victory and the Agony of Defeat

Remember that sports video, *The Thrill of Victory and the Agony of Defeat*? The first part shows the victorious athletes—track stars raising their arms in celebration, swimmers touching the wall—backed by all this great music that reminded me of *Rocky* and how you could be somebody. Then all of a sudden the music changes to this death dirge, and they show this skier coming flying down the hill and *whup!* wipe out. I mean, *wipe* out, do three or four flips—*phoomp, phoomp, phoomp* —go through a fence, *bam!* and then off the side of the mountain. Then the announcer comes on and says, in a funereal voice, "The agony of defeat." I guarantee you, nobody remembers the victorious athletes in that video, but we all remember the guy who crashed and burned. When it comes to dating, that guy who went off the side of the mountain is me.

Dating is a lot like sports. You have to practice, you work out, you study the greats, you hope to make the team, and it hurts to be cut from the squad. The big difference between dating and sports is that in sports you can make up for lack of ability with ambition, or "heart," as it is called. The coach always uses the player with heart as an example to the talented players when they aren't playing up to their potential. "Guys, I wish I had eight players like Eddy, here. He's small, can't run, can't jump, can't shoot, basically can't play —but he never gives up. I can count on Eddy to give me 150 percent. He has heart." In actuality, the coach wishes the other guys would play harder so he could cut Eddy.

I had heart. I would hang in there until I could meet that one special woman who would love me for myself. I mean, with all these billions of women out there and only so many men to go around—women are always complaining about the shortage of real men—why couldn't I have just one? Come on, God, just one. Doesn't even have to be one of your best ones. If she has most of her vital organs, I'll be happy, Lord. *Just one! Please!*

That was then. Now, I know guys who have that one special woman—fine as wine, as we used to say. What more could a man want? MORE! This is where men and women differ. Women sit around and say, "I would be happy just to find a good guy. That's all I want." (Good means please have a job and rich wouldn't be bad.) They want a quality man. Men, we want quantity. Now, don't get me wrong, we start off looking for quality and then get greedy. I personally believe it has something to do with God taking a rib from us in the

Garden of Eden; we are not complete. All right, that's a stretch, I was just trying to make us look a little less doggish. But the truth is that eventually, no matter how gaga you and your woman are over each other, inside your inner ear, getting louder and louder, you will start to hear that sound: *click-clack-click-clack-click-click-clack*—the sound of the high heels of all those other women out there who are walking past your door and passing you by.

See, guys have no reference point for dating just one woman. The married man on all sitcoms is the dope, the butt of all the jokes, Mr. Dummy. The best he can hope for is to be the best friend of the star of the sitcom, the single guy. The only exception was the Cosby show, but that was different because Bill Cosby was older. He had teenage children, so he had to have one woman to help fight back if the kids ganged up on them. But most movie heroes, like James Bond, Our Man Flint, Superman, never had just one girlfriend. (Technically it was Clark Kent, not Superman, who wanted one woman, Lois Lane. But, nooooo, Clark wasn't good enough for Lois—too goofy. I've always thought Lois must have been pretty ditzy if she couldn't tell Clark was Superman just because he wore glasses. You have to admit that was the cheapest undercover disguise known to man. Even the Lone Ranger had a mask, and cowboys have no budget for costumes.)

A man's first dating fumbles brand him for life, creating a scorecard for future relationships with women. It's a rare man who doesn't get kicked to the

curb over and over in the beginning. That's why I hate
to see kids today not only start to take the opposite sex
seriously but actually fall in love at such a young age. I
didn't even contemplate dating until I turned thirteen
or fourteen—the hormones kicked in at twelve but I
didn't understand. By then our kids are already emo-
tionally scarred. The other day I was listening to my
son tell his friend about how he was depressed because
his woman left him. He's seven years old! What
woman? You don't have a "woman" at age seven, and
you have too many toys to play with to be depressed.
He said, "Dad, you just don't understand—love hurts."
Well, yeah! That's why, when I was seven, you let a girl
know you liked her by beating her up, pulling her hair,
knocking her off the slide, throwing sand in her face.
Puppy love, we called it. Now kids skip the puppy-
chow years and go straight to kibbles and bits.

I was traumatized at my first dance in junior high
school. They called them "Coke" dances, I guess because they had free Coca-Cola for all the kids at the
dance. The drinks came in two-ounce cups, so you had
to drink about 200 of them to quench your young thirst.
We were goofy at that age, so only the really cool guys
actually danced. Most of those guys are in jail now.
Don't want to get cool too fast, you get cool burnout—
makes you do crazy things. But my buddies told me
that Linda, this girl I liked, wanted to dance with me,
and so I had to get up the nerve.

I was psyched! My heart started racing, I started
sweating Coke out of my pores as I went off to ask her.
I was moving in slow motion, and all the eyes in the
gym were on me. "Will he make it?" "Will she tell him
yes?" So much drama for a young man. It is memories

like this that make me worry for my kids when I allow them to start dating—at the age of twenty-six.

When I reached Linda, all her friends were giggling and pointing at me. I thought I had the seal of approval, so I even started walking cooler—as cool as you can in tight, highwater pants my mama just got off a five-year layaway. I stood in front of Linda and started to mumble incoherently, "Um . . . LLLii . . . um . . . do   you . . . um . . . Linnn . . . um . . . would you . . . do you . . . do you wanna dance?" Right then the music, which had been blaring, stopped. Everything that had been moving in slow motion became real time as Linda shouted out, "Not with you!"

My buddies had set me up! It was the cruelest trick anyone could play on a newbie to dating. Stunned, I did the walk of shame back over to where my coat was, then I ran out of the gym. The only reason I ever went back to school to face the ridicule was that my mama made me.

There were rules to dating back then, the most important one being you had to meet the father. Today there are no fathers around to meet, or they are in another city—no pressure there. At some point a girl would say, "My father wants to meet you," and she would always lie about the volatility of his personality. "My dad is cool. He's going to like you." Yeah, right.

I was rightfully scared to death at my first father meeting. Regina's (you do know these are fake names, don't you?) dad had a bad rep among the fellas, so I made sure I got to her house before her father got home from work. That way, if he looked crazy, I could act like I was just leaving and only have minimal contact.

Now, most of the fathers in my hometown were hard-working factory men who wore coveralls and steel-toed boots, which they would not hesitate one moment to plant squarely in your butt if you messed over their baby girls. Regina's mother was so nice—bad sign! The nicer the mother, the crazier the father is. When he came into the house he looked mad already, and Regina and her mother ran out of the room. They left me *alone.*

I just sat there in the living room as he got his dinner from the kitchen and proceeded to eat it in front of the TV, just looking at me every now and then and grunting. I couldn't quite make out the words he was saying, so I would just nod and say yes at the pauses. Suddenly he stopped grunting and, with the diction of James Earl Jones, asked, "Aren't you Reverend Adkins' son?" Yes, I acknowledged. Then the worst thing happened. A smile came across his face as he said, "I know your father. Good man. I know I don't have to worry about you."

Don't have to worry about you. Those words cut me like a knife. What was I, a eunuch? I didn't want the father to trust me totally—that would mean I had no cool. He was calling Regina into the room. "Why can't you meet more boys like him?" Now he had gone too far. I should have stood up and French-kissed her right in front of him. He would have beat me down, but I would have had my dignity.

For the rest of my teenage years, I was dogged by the trust of fathers. They would give me letters of recommendation for other fathers, reading, "He is harmless." I became so tight with some of the fathers that after the girl and I had broken up, they would still want to see me. Some of them still call me to this day. Yuck! This suffocating trust continued to haunt me in college.

Harmless, good guy, you can trust him, just like a brother to me. These are the terms women use to describe the guy who is their buddy, not the guy they desire or have fantasies about. You are so harmless that if you tried to get intimate with one of your girl "buddies," she would say, "What are you doing, silly? I don't look at you that way. You are my friend, you big teddy bear." *Argggh!* I felt like Charlie Brown. Now, your male buddies don't know that you aren't "getting with" any of these girls you hang around. As a matter of fact, they think you are getting with all of them. You are a player. They are asking you to hook them up! Or worse yet, one of your girl buddies is asking you to hook her up with one of your male friends. *I HATE THAT!*

But the ultimate worst was when the fellas and the ladies were hanging out talking about me—the guys wanting to know why the girls could kick it with Sinbad and not with them. "Sinbad is so nice and *doesn't want anything*," the girls would say. My cover was blown! I had to do some quick damage control, which by this time I was good at, being a master liar. "Guys, they were messing with your head. Hey, even your ladies act like y'all aren't getting busy, don't they?" This slowed them down for a while, but it was a close call. I spread some rumors about a couple of the girls and me, just to keep my credibility. I know it was wrong, but they left me no choice.

The most painful part of being "the good guy" is that girls disrespected the laws of nature when they were around me. I stayed in the dorm on the floor with all the other basketball players—lots of testosterone. Every once in a while one of the guys and his lady would have a falling-out in the middle of the night, and the girl would come to my room because the word was out that I was a "good guy." She'd cry on my shoulder, then she would ask could she sleep there with me. I'd be thinking, "All right!" Then right when I was about to make my move, she would say, "Can I call Bobby? I want him to know where I am."

"Why?"

"Just in case he wants me to come back . . ."

"WHAT? No, you can't call Bobby. What kind of man do you think I am?" That's what I wanted to say. What I said was, "The phone is under that pillow, go ahead and use it. Dial 9 first . . ." Then, to add insult to injury, the girl would actually take off her clothes and snuggle up next to me in some flimsy nightie, saying, "You are so nice. Thanks for letting me stay here. You ought to have a girlfriend." *Chump!*

Now I was getting worried. It was okay to be naive in high school, but not as naive as I was. For years I took my basketball with me everywhere—not the best ice breaker with girls. I would put him in the front seat of my car, strap the seat belt around him and make my friends ride in the back—they hated that, especially the girls, but it was better than walking. At the movies he would sit beside me: "Is that seat free?" "No, can't you see that's my basketball's seat?" I would even give my basketballs names, and bury them when they died —too slick to palm anymore. Eli was my favorite basketball: He was the new Spalding indoor/outdoor model, one of the first. He died in combat—got hit by a car after a bad jump shot. But enough about Eli. I've already been through plenty of therapy over his sudden and tragic death.

So it was kind of a shock to be at the movies not with a basketball but with a girl. I had invited her to see the basketball flick *Cornbread, Earl and Me*—the perfect date movie, right? But since I'd already seen it twenty times, I knew I wouldn't miss anything if I tried to get busy at what every teenager knows the movies are for—to try to cop a feel. The trouble was, I didn't have the moves down yet. I was trying that yawn-stretch-put-your-arm-around-the-date maneuver I'd seen guys do, but I kept misjudging the distance and smacking her in the head. Finally she got so frustrated with my inept attempts that she just took my arm and dragged it over her shoulder. *Whew! Mission accomplished!* I was grateful, but when she leaned back on my arm, she hit my funny bone, so I kept having spasms against the back of her head: "Don't be fresh!" "Uh-uh . . . Sorry . . . uh . . ." But I wasn't going to let that discourage me. I was determined, no matter how scared I got, to force myself to touch her breasts.

I was ready. I was also so nervous that I was sweating profusely, dripping on her blouse. Tremble by tremble, inch by inch—I touched it! I started fondling and caressing it. I was in heaven. I was even bold enough to look over at her. She had this look on her face that I thought was ecstasy. (I later found out it was pain.) It was my first feel! I was the man!

When we came out of the movie, she kept rubbing her elbow. "What's wrong?" I asked. "Did it fall asleep?"

"No," she said, "it hurts from you rubbing it during the whole movie. You are strange. I want you to take me home now so I can soak it in Epsom salts."

I was so embarrassed, I never called her again. She had a big mouth, too—other girls at school would rub their elbows whenever they saw me, acting like they were in pain.

But that was not my most embarrassing moment. That moment came later, when I was in college, one Friday night when I was hanging out at a club in Denver called Lucky's, with my friends and fellow ballplayers Bobby and Tootie. Bobby had met a girl who agreed to eat breakfast with him if he could find guys for her two roommates—the old "I-can't-leave-my-friends" routine. So Bobby got me and Tootie, implying that the ladies might be interested in more than breakfast. Another guy might have been excited, but all I could think was: "I'm busted . . ."

See, Bobby and Tootie didn't know I was a little behind when it came to being with the ladies, because I talked such a good game. Every weekend we would go out to "score"—to me, that meant making it through the night without having to actually back up all that trash I talked; to have the fellas see me get a woman's phone number and then act like I was mad because she didn't take me home. "Man, that girl is a trip, guys. All talk and no action. Let's get out of here." I was at an age where the love stakes were pretty high, when people just assumed that you were at a certain level in the game. I almost felt that if I hadn't hooked up with a woman by now, it would be too clumsy and awkward to try to learn. I was still a rookie at love—no, not even a rookie; I was still in the locker room.

But how could I confess the truth to the guys—that I was still a virgin, especially after all those lies I floated? Then it came to me: I had to be James, James Bond. James was always down with the women—always in control, never had to question. He never lost his cool, even when he was about to die. What James was all about, I now realized, was staying cool until he could figure out a way to fake the funk. At the moments in *Goldfinger* when the laser was coming up between James's legs, when Oddjob's hat was flying at his neck, he didn't even flinch. That's the point I was at now, not knowing whether to bob, weave, or just spin. And I got an inspiration—to sit next to the ugliest girl, then act mad that Bobby and Tootie had gotten the good ones. Faking it.

We were meeting the girls at Denny's down the street. The Denny's chain must see more action than any other restaurants in the world because they're usually the only thing open that late—pickup hours. Everyone from the homeless to movie moguls to pimps is there eating that nasty food with the same hope of getting lucky. And it looked like we were going to—my girl was getting all lovey-dovey even before the menus came. My plan had been shot—none of the girls were ugly, they were fine, fine, and fine. What would James do? I know: "I'll be really rude and then she won't want to be with me. They'll have that girltalk in the bathroom and decide that none of them can stand me and they'll cut me loose."

Just my luck: I had picked a girl with a high abuse threshold. There was nothing I could say—not about her hair, the way she ate, what she ordered: "The Grand Slam breakfast! Looks like I got stuck with the greedy one"—that could drive her off. I'm not proud of my behavior, but she had to be hungry or broke or both to have stayed at that table. Bobby and Tootie were looking at me like I was crazy.

The check came: put-up-or-shut-up time. I was like an animal in a cage: What would James do? I excused myself to go to the bathroom, and once there, I climbed out the window. I ran the four miles back to the campus—not an easy job in those seventies platform shoes —hoping that Bobby and Tootie weren't looking for me in the car. When they finally came knocking at my door at five o'clock in the morning, I was ready. I went off on them for leaving me at Denny's: "If you didn't want me with you, you should have told me. How could you just ditch me like that, man?" By the time I was done, they were apologizing. My secret was safe. Another victory snatched from the jaws of defeat. Or just the opposite—I'm not sure.

The whole man-woman relationship was different in the seventies. Nowadays even young boys are players. The girls don't make these boys work hard—men get lazy if not pushed to work hard—and then wonder why they are getting dogged. In the seventies you had to be crazy to give a girl your number like she was going to call you first. Her mother would go off on her. "I know you are not calling that boy. Don't be so anxious, make him call *you* first. You'll sound desperate, child." In fact, if the 1970s had a theme song it would be "Ain't Too Proud to Beg," by my boys, the Temptations. Every song was about begging: begging for forgiveness, begging a woman to return your love, begging for one more chance. For men, begging was an art.

Today everybody gets right to the "Can you spend the night?" question. In the seventies you couldn't spend the night because you still lived at home—too many people in the house. And there were no beepers, E-mail, Internet, cellular phones, or things to help avoid the personal contact back then. You spent a lot of *face-to-face* time. Even answering machines were just coming in. They only held about ten minutes' worth of messages, but that was plenty—who was going to listen longer than that? The messages were very basic: "I am not home, leave a message after the beep," then you had to wait for this long five-minute beep to end. Sometimes I would just hang up the phone. And what you said on them was just as basic: "Huh, I hope this thing is working. Umm, I will call you when you are home, bye." There was no call-waiting, so if the phone was busy, you had to ride over there and talk face to face. Lots of time for talking and begging.

My worst begging experience, I didn't even know I was begging. There is nothing sadder than being an extra spoke in a wheel, except for not knowing you are the extra spoke. I took Gayle, the girl who would become my official first date in life, to a movie and we got some pizza—a small step for mankind but a giant step for me. She was, and probably still is, fine, sexy, and nice, but the thing that appealed to me the most was her sense of humor. Gayle could crack me up—she would make my stomach hurt with some of the stuff she did.

Turned out, I wasn't the only one she made laugh. She also made Joe laugh. Joe, who was one year ahead of me in school and played football, was cool; we got along great, maybe too great. The problem was, we both liked Gayle—or, well, it was no problem for him. I was the Special Ed student in this situation. I would call Gayle to ask if I could come by, and she would say, "Sure, would you bring some pizza?" I would go get some pizza and fly on over to Gayle's house in my family's van—not a passenger van, mind you, but a tricked-out van with an eight-track tape player—playing the theme song from the movie *The Mack* all the way.

Well, when I got to the house, Joe would be sitting in the living room. So I'd play it cool and exchange some dap with Joe. For those of you who don't know, *dapping* is the way brothers would greet each other in the seventies—a series of complicated handshakes and fist taps that, according to the area of the country you were from, took anywhere from a few seconds to fifteen minutes to complete. Fifteen minutes . . . Not only did I have to dap with the brother, but Joe started eating Gayle's and my pizza, like I was the delivery boy from Domino's. He even had the nerve to eat my special Canadian bacon–pepperoni combo slice that I had never before shared with man or woman!

On top of that, I now had to play the waiting game—which one of us would outlast the other and get Gayle alone? How could I know the game was stacked against me from the beginning? We were one big, happy family, enjoying conversation and pizza, when the setup came: Gayle, my friend, said, "Sinbad, I ran out of pop"—that's soda to you East Coast people—"Would you mind running to the store to get some more?" Seemed innocent enough, seeing as how Joe didn't have a car. I did about seventy miles an hour going to the corner store, all the while thinking of ways to get rid of Joe when I got back. I made it back to the house in under fifteen minutes, a new record for shopping, but something was wrong in Mudville—DUH! All the lights were out when I got back. I'm thinking, "Power outage—no, the rest of the neighborhood has lights." So I punched the doorbell—*ring, ring-ring-ring-ring-ring-ring-ring.* I rang for half an hour. Then it hit me— the extra spoke; I was the extra spoke. I dropped the pops on the porch—I didn't want Gayle and Joe to be parched from any extracurricular activity, and I'm not talking Twister, either—and I walked cool to my van.

Well, so much for my girls-go-for-guys-with-cars theory.

I drove away dazed and confused: Where did I go wrong? How could I have been so stupid? James Bond would not have gone to the store—he would have given the other guy the keys to his car and said, "I brought the pizza, you get the pop, sucker!" Alas, I am not Bond, but Bad—Sinbad, that is. I would like to say that this was a learning experience and end my story here, but I must be honest: I let Gayle lose me seven more times—each scheme more devious than the last —until I finally gave up. A man can only share so much pizza.

To this day I can't order pizza: too many memories. Gayle, wherever you are, I hope whenever you order or eat a pizza, you think of me—while you choke. I am not bitter. I hope the cheese burns a hole through the roof of your mouth and they have no water. I am not mad. And the crust gets wedged in your esophagus. I feel no pain.

Kicked to the curb . . .

Let me tell you a parable: Two men have been lost in the desert for five days and are dying of thirst. A stranger shows up on the horizon, and he has camels and water. The first thirsty man sees him and starts crying out, "Help me, help me. I am dying of thirst. Please, I must have water." The second man, equally thirsty, says nothing. As the stranger walks over, thirsty man number one starts reaching for the water flask and acting a fool for the water. Man number two says nothing, and the stranger is intrigued. All the while the first man is crying out, "Water, water, I must have water," the stranger is walking past him to man number two. "Are you not thirsty?" he asks. "Very much so," replies the second man. "Then why do you not cry out for water like your friend here?" "Because the water belongs to you, stranger. If you choose to share it with us, I will not have to ask." "I see," says the stranger, and he proceeds to let him drink from his flask. The first thirsty man is totally confused and angrily asks, "Did you not hear me ask for water?" "Yes, I did," replies the stranger. "I don't understand. Why did you walk past me to help my friend?" "Because your needs were showing," says the stranger. *"What?"* "You made it clear what you needed before I was off my camel—water, not medical attention, it seemed— so I could give water to you at any time. But your friend was quiet. I didn't know what condition he was in. I had to go to him."

Men and women, the opposite sex can tell when your needs are showing. That's why they have the power—because we can never tell when their needs are showing because they have self-control. I have to admit, some of the best times I have had with the opposite sex were when I was still naive. I miss the harmless puppy-love stage, although I think women are glad we got past throwing sand in their eyes. Believe it or not, I even miss the "scared of it" stage during my college years. There was something about that fear, that adrenaline rush, the running away—I especially enjoyed the running; it became a game, a challenge. I will never have that control again because now "my needs are showing." All my life I have heard the saying "The squeaky wheel gets the grease"—not always. Sometimes the loud wheel is passed over for one a little more quiet and relaxing.

I know what you're thinking: "How can your needs not show when it is love at first sight?" Ain't no such animal—there is no love at first sight. And what do you mean by it, exactly? You saw a woman putting gas in her car and you knew you were in love? Maybe it was the gas fumes, fool. There are so many variables to consider in this situation—for one, the distance of the so-called *sighting*. If you wear glasses or contacts, you can barely see the car up ahead of you on the road, let alone love. Three to six feet is the ideal distance for love-at-first-sight striking. But, guys, how many women do you know who let strange men get that close? Only in an aerobics class can strangers of the opposite sex get that close, but the body odors can get in the way of the love *thang*. You might think it's love when it's just the funk talking to you, baby brother. Realistically, what are the chances that it's love at first sight?

Another example: Men, how many times have you seen a fine woman on the other side of the street and almost got yourself killed trying to cross the street to get to her—only to find out "she" is a "he" with long hair? We've all been there—Fantasyland. People who *think* they fall in love at first sight live in a fantasy world: "Promise me we'll never argue." Yeah, dream on.

I believe more in love at first *fight* than love at first sight. Have you ever met somebody for the first time and somehow, right off the bat, you get into an argument? You leave the encounter talking about how much you couldn't stand him/her, then you run into the person again and something magical happens? So many people who can't stand each other when they first meet wind up falling in love and getting married—but why? I believe it happens because there is nowhere to go but up in that relationship.

If you listen to the scientists, attraction is all a matter of our pheromones. Your body gives off these chemical sexual signals. I think they also attract roaches. Which means, if a woman is attracted to you, she won't want to stay at your place because you'll have roaches.

If you're serious about somebody and thinking marriage, you should definitely check out their family and background. It is a good idea for a woman to be careful and do some checking. For instance, I bet a lot of you women are dating, or are even married to, ex–*pee-pee boys* and don't even have a clue. When we were growing up—no matter where you grew up, I don't care if it was New York, Detroit, Tennessee—every elementary school had a pee-pee boy, a boy who smelled like pee. He could never get to the bathroom in time and he'd just stand there every time as that look came over his face.

"Aw, Pee-Pee, not again!"

"I didn't pee. I'm just sweating."

That's why you've got to check out your man's history. Go back to his old elementary school. "Do you remember a LeRoy Johnson?"

"*Pee-Pee* Johnson? That boy still alive? We thought he had peed himself to death."

And men, you've got to be careful too. We've all been with women, particularly in the disco days, who are dancing away and their face starts coming off because they start sweating. You spin around and when you're back facing her you wonder: "I had a fine woman dancing here a second ago, where did this *creature* come from?"

The dating scene is different in every decade. Women in their teens and twenties are real romantic. In their thirties, they're more realistic. And by the time they get to their forties, they're practically to the point of pain. They've been hurt. You ask a woman for her phone number and she screams. "NO!! I DON'T HAVE A NUMBER. A MAN LIKE YOU RAN UP MY PHONE BILL AND I DON'T HAVE A PHONE NOW!"

Some women try to black out of their mind the men they've had. "No, I've never had anybody. I've been taking care of myself . . . Oh, who, them? . . . They're my children . . . I don't know where they came from . . . They're just all over the house, I can't stop them."

Women when they get serious about you will try to dominate your time so they can separate you from your friends. You can see the TV nature show: "Today, the human female is hunting the human male. You can tell that those are the males over there. They're the stupid-looking ones. Watch the female now. She's zeroed in on the slowest, weakest male . . . She's now going to lure the male away from the pack . . . Now she's got him on his own . . . She'll toy with him for a while, and then, when she's tired of that, she'll bring him down."

Listen to her now: "Oh, you just bring joy to my life . . . Why, to be with you brings brightness to my face."

And he's tripping, like, "Hey, this is cool!" He asks her, "Baby, what do you want to do?"

"Oh, whatever, as long as it's with you."

"You wanna go to the movies?"

"If I can just sit next to you and be with you. That's all I desire." Then they're sitting in the movies and he asks her, "You want some popcorn?"

"I'll just sit here and lick the butter from your fingertips."

He's thinking, "I'm the man now!" Pretty soon, he'll be standing up in front of the preacher or the judge and going "I do."

And she's going "I do"—but before those two words are quite out of her mouth, her whole voice drops down as her head whips around, her eyes bearing down on him, and without skipping a beat, she spouts, "SOME THINGS GONNA CHANGE AROUND HERE! I DON'T THINK I LIKE YOUR ATTITUDE!"

•   •   •

nce you become the father of a daughter, the whole game changes—you see everything about dating differently. Because now you have to dog and criticize everything that you thought was cool when you did it—even (especially) if you're still doing it. You tell your daughter to watch out for all the doggish guys out there, that ninety percent of the men in the world only want one thing—sound like anyone you know? Fathers are the biggest hypocrites around.

I know the first time I let my daughter go on a date, it is going to kill me inside with worry. But if things are the same as when I was growing up, she's already been going out for a year—this is just the first guy normal enough to bring home. You tell your daughter to wait and find the right man. But in your heart you know she is not listening to you. What could you possibly know about being young and in love? You wish you could tell her exactly how much you know, but that would only give her ammunition to use later on: "Daddy, you said you did the same thing at my age. Why can't I?" Never let your children know all about your past. Be selective about which stories you share—they don't need to hear a word about kissing or intimate contact.

To get ready for when my daughter starts dating, I have been going to the shooting range so I can pick off any boy who tries to hurt her from one hundred yards away. And along with some other fathers who are skilled in weaponry and martial arts, I have just started a neighborhood watch group to protect the intended victims (our daughters). We are putting on a fund-raiser this summer to raise money for a local dojo and shooting range to help train the less experienced fathers—you know, just trying to give something back to the community. We've adapted the philosophy of Genghis Khan—"Give a man a fish, and he eats for a day; teach a man to fish and he eats for a lifetime"—for our slogan: "Show a teenage boy a gun—and he'll have your daughter home before 11:30." Great words from a great man. A simple father like the rest of us.

Our group is going to enforce the kind of rules fathers imposed on us when we dated their daughters: Each violation of section 13-a of the daughter protection code has a specified punishment: Loud radio—shoot out the tires of the offender. Blow the horn instead of coming inside—shoot out the windshield; second offense punishable by death. Pull up in a van—nuke 'em: That one's nonnegotiable. I added it because we had a van, and I know the damage that can be done. I didn't do any—I was Mr. Let's Get Some Pizza and Talk—but my brother Mark: Well, let's just say you're lucky I never told Mom, Mark; and don't forget, it's not too late to tell her now. Our watch group already has its system in place. Every house with a daughter of dating age in it has a panic button—a sort of silent alarm to let us know the enemy is coming. Should a perpetrator of violations try to escape, a father hits the button and —*boom!* we're all there, with more than enough firepower to stop him. It may take a village to raise a child, but it takes a well-trained cadre of well-armed men to protect our daughters from the dogs out there. Don't worry: We are ready.

Waiting to *Inhale*

For all the tons of books and hours of TV talk shows all you women gobble up trying to better understand us men, who would have thought that it would be a novel and then, especially, the movie based on that novel that would become such a big phenomenon for all of you to discuss, discuss, discuss some more at your sister groups? Yes, I'm talking about Terry McMillan's *Waiting to Exhale.*

Well, girlfriends, I'm here to tell you that most men, including myself, and a lot of my female compatriots felt sorry for any woman who identified with those women in the movie. You know the sisters I am talking about.

"Girlfriend, I felt that movie was my *autobiography.*"

If that sounds like you, you had better start some

inhaling. Let's get some oxygen to your brain! I'll start you off: Ready? Okay, inhale—*Fffwuppp!*

Do you really think that movie was real life? I have never seen four women that happy to be together in my life. There should have been a fight *somewhere* in that movie. I was waiting for the fight, or at least a decent wig-whipping-off argument.

Right in the beginning, the woman's getting dressed to go to a party and is putting the final touches on her makeup. Her husband says, "Do you feel like going to this party?"

She replies, "Not really." Now here comes the bogus part: He proceeds to nonchalantly tell her, "Good, then stay home because I am taking the white woman I've been sleeping with and am leaving you for."

Now, I am waiting for gunplay because this is the boldest move by a man in the history of film. James Bond couldn't have pulled this off. This is a move you make on the phone, from Jamaica, *after* you have gotten all of your stuff out of the house, got your car—the Mercedes, not the Taurus—and emptied the bank account.

I was tripping enough already when he made an even dumber move. He told her that he would be *back for his things in a couple of days*—like she was going to pack for him while he was gone. And he left the Mercedes and took the Ford Taurus. DUMB! I hated this guy more than the women sitting next to me screaming at the screen, "DOG! DOG! KILL HIM!" I started shouting the same thing with them, that's how mad he made me. It would have been better for men around the world if he had died early on in this flick.

Then there's the burning of his car and stuff the

next day. I personally think this was a dangerous scene to show to women. Some woman got jacked up trying to do this to her man after watching the movie. In real life, if you burn up a man's car, clothes, and watches, even if he left them there, you had better already be on your way to your mom's house. No man is going to check out his burned-up heap of stuff and go, "Girl, what did you do?" It's obvious, she burned them up.

Now, me, I would shout,

"ARE YOU READY TO RRRRUMBLE?!?!"

. . . and it would be on! You thought the Great Chicago Fire was big—it would look like amateur night at the Apollo. As a matter of fact, that fire would still be burning. They would have to change the name of the movie from *Waiting to Exhale* to *Burn, Baby, Burn.* I can hear the Babyface soundtrack now, a remix of "Disco Inferno." *"Burn baby burn, disco inferno, burn baby burn, burn this mother down . . ."*

I Did

Ah, marriage! It's a lovely institution, but it affects men and women differently. Women take on a glow, but men get brain-damaged. As soon as a man gets married, the brain gets sucked right out of his head. *Thwuup!!* It's *gone.* If someone would tell you that a woman who has not known you nearly as long as you've known your own family was gonna come and change your life *totally*, well, you would hoot them down. "You're crazy, man!" But it's a fact and you can't fight it.

Now, ladies, I'm sorry if this chapter seems a little bit chauvinistic. But you've got enough books, let's face it—*Smart Women, Foolish Choices; Men Are from Mars, Women Are from Venus* (I know a man wrote it but it's still for you); *How to Marry a Rich Man; The 100 Biggest Lies Men Tell; Waiting to Exhale* . . . So I thought it was time to write a little something just for the guys—something to keep their brain cells and hope alive—something to help them survive this marriage thing.

I'm not saying marriage doesn't work for some people. Look at my mother and father—they've been married for years. But there are things you must prepare yourself for. The vows are just the beginning. They should have Rod Serling come out during the ceremony and announce, "You are about to take a journey not of sight and sound, to a realm where logic and reason seldom meet . . . Welcome to the *Twilight Zone*."

Now, for the first step on that journey: Forget those big dreams of fairy-tale weddings, $5,000 designer cake, horse-drawn carriage, and first-class honeymoon in Hawaii. I say if you must have all that, at least wait until you've been married five years. No, six. Actually, make it eight, so you can see if that famous seven-year itch is still making either one of you scratch. There's nothing sadder than breaking up two years after one of those monster weddings and having to pawn the old gifts because you have wedding payments still due.

If the engagement holds up, pay attention during the planning stages. Watch your in-laws. If they insist on controlling who comes and who doesn't come to the wedding and what's on the program, you know you're in for trouble. Let them run the wedding and there will be pushy in-laws ruling your marriage roost down the road. Now, if your in-laws are worth millions, then thank them for caring and do everything they say. If they're not rich, tell them to butt out.

You women all want that big old engagement ring,

don't you? You can't wait to walk around so all your friends are going, "Oooh, girl, he must *love* you." No, it doesn't mean he loves you. It means brain damage is setting in. I'll tell you this, when a woman's got my giant diamond on her finger, if we break up she better not fall asleep. Because even if it means I've got to cut off her finger, I will be getting my ring back. I'm sorry —but that's a car payment. Or a car!

That's why I believe you should buy a cubic zirconium for an engagement ring. But don't stay out in the sun too long; it will melt. Later on—say, nine or ten years down the road if you're still married—you can buy her the real thing. She will have earned it.

There are things that you will not know about your woman until you get married because single women almost never let you see them in their natural state. Then, one day, they get married and they just quit all that. They wake up and announce that you're going to see them as they really are, no makeup. "Aaah!! That's not my wife! What have you done to my wife? This woman looks possessed!"

Now, while the wife may have changed her appearance in the morning, the husband has an even more startling turn of events ahead of him. He *disappears*. No, not into the witness protection program, I'm talking about how his buddies will invariably drive around to his usual prenuptial stomping grounds and find no trace of him anywhere. Then, one day, soon after, they will spot the new husband around the mall. He doesn't even remember their names. He's just sitting on a bench, holding a woman's coat and a purse, just sort of twitching. "Hey, man," his buddies will yell out, "it's us, remember?"

The husband chirps up all bright and singsongy like a four-year-old, "My wife is inside shopping. I hold her purse so she doesn't have to hold it. It's got all my money in it. She keeps it for me. Isn't she sweet to do that so that I don't have to worry?" That's it, we've lost him.

What's worse, men, is that you will see when you're married that suddenly people don't speak to *you* anymore, they speak to your wife. You'll be standing there, and they'll come over *to her*—"How's he doing? Tell him we said hello." You just stand there all sad and confused, going, "Hunh?"

You can tell a married man because he's always apologizing. And usually, he doesn't even know what he's apologizing for. He gets that way because he cannot outargue his wife. It's an impossibility. One of the saddest sights you'll ever see is when two cars have stopped at a stoplight, both with a husband and wife in the front seat. In one car, the man is looking away from his screaming wife with a look of beaten-down, quiet desperation in his eyes. In the other car, the husband can't even enjoy the momentary lull in his car, he feels so sorry for the other guy he's watching in the first car, but his almost equally sorrowful long face says, "I can't jump in and help you, brother. You're on your own. I'm barely hanging on myself."

That is so embarrassing—to be arguing with your wife in the car. She has the complete advantage, and she knows it because you're trying to concentrate on driving. You didn't know the argument was going to happen, but she knew it when she left the house. She was just saving up her start for the most inconvenient time.

Women don't get mad at you about something you *just* did. They have a special memory just for arguing that goes back twenty or thirty years. I'm talking *precision* memory, for everything you've ever done around her: the time, date, place, what you wore and how it fit you, what you said and your hand position when you said it. She just files away everything automatically in this mental computer and unlike a regular computer, this memory will never crash, it probably keeps ticking after she does. You finally bury her in her grave and from six feet under you'll hear this muffled shout, "AT THE CHURCH PICNIC, 1985, WHAT KIND OF LOOK WAS THAT YOU GAVE KENESHA, MISTER BIG EYES!!"

Man, you will be sitting with your woman and you're worrying that maybe she's found out about something you just did, only you can't think what it is. What you don't realize, you poor fool, is that *whoosh!* she's just had a *flashback*—comes up out of nowhere, maybe something she sees on TV, and she explodes, "OH, YES!! 1985, JUNE SIXTEENTH. WHATCHU GOT TO SAY ABOUT THAT?!?!"

You, you've lied so much since then, you barely remember what you lied about *yesterday*, so you have no idea what has set her off or how to respond. Trust me, it will end quicker if you don't try.

If you learn nothing else about marriage, men, you must remember this:

SHUT UP

Men, just shut up. I can't repeat this often enough. Your words will be used against you, not in a court of law—ha! the meanest judge in the world could not be as hard on you as your wife can be every day of your life in the trial of your marriage.

All the marriage books tell you that marriage is about making "compromises." That's about as believable as the brochure for your honeymoon. There are no real compromises in marriage. If you're driving the raggedy car, it's because she's driving the good car. If you're going to the movie she loves and you hate, that's no compromise.

Oh, when you first get married your wife may try to make you think she's being very patient and accommodating. Right! On the weekend, when all you want to do, been looking forward to it all week, is kick back and watch the game, she will try to talk to you before the game comes on. "Can I just talk to you?"

"Aw, baby, I'm trying to watch the game."

She actually turns and leaves the room and you think all your older married friends were wrong and soon they'll be coming to you for advice on how to handle their women. You are the king of your castle. Hah! You're nothing but a lowly serf. Because two seconds before the final buzzer of what is now a tie game, Jordan's got the ball—*click*—"Can I talk to you now?"

"You couldn't have waited two seconds until the game was over?"

"IS THIS GAME MORE IMPORTANT THAN OUR RELATIONSHIP?"

Don't answer that question. Bite your tongue until blood comes out your nose, if you have to, but shut up! If you watch somebody who is a successful marriage veteran in this kind of "game" situation you will learn the man's ideal defense: "Yes . . . yes, dear . . .

That's right, sweetheart . . . I'm stupid, yes . . .
You're so right, so right . . ." She's got nothing left to
argue about at the moment, so she turns and walks out
of the room. *Click*—he's watching the game in peace
and quiet.

So, a married man *can* get some time to himself
inside his own home, but if he wants to go outside on
his own—not so fast. All you single men, when y'all
want to go somewhere you just get up and go. A married man's got to plan his strategy of how to get out of
the house two to three years in advance. Even a simple
trip to get to the mall, buy some tools, sneak them into
the house, will take a minimum hundred hours of planning the breakout and return and favorable weather
conditions on the big day.

Your single friends don't understand that you just
can't come and go as in your carefree, unattached days
and they will get you in trouble when they say they'll
meet you somewhere but they forget and come to pick
you up at your house—just as your wife turns the corner into your drive.

"Excuse me, where do you think you're going?" Immediately, you're six years old again, stammering, your
voice all squeaky, "See . . . umm . . . see, Bobby
. . . see they called me . . . and Bobby . . .
Bobby asked if I wanted to go play basketball . . . I
said I don't know if I really want to go . . . They just
sort of stopped by anyway . . . but I told them it
didn't matter, I couldn't go without asking my wife.
Can I go? You said I should be getting some more fresh
air. We'll be right across the street. You'll be able to
see me out the window. When it gets dark, I'll come
back in as soon as you call me, I promise."

For pure show performance during your marriage, though, I don't think anything can beat the "walk home" threat. Women pull out this major move when you're out somewhere and get into a fight. They will storm out of the room, crying, "I CAN'T TAKE ANY MORE!! I'M GONNA WALK HOME, I'M GONNA WALK HOME!"

You stand up and start a slow "married man's jog." You don't really want to catch her, you just want to keep her in sight. If she keeps going, you follow her in the car, calling out, "Baby, please get in."

She's still acting. "NO! You don't care! You just don't care."

Now, I don't care what that woman says, don't let her walk home. If you let that woman walk home, just keep on driving. Start a new life somewhere else, but do not go home.

If you do let her walk home, you better play stupid to save yourself. As you can see, if you're going to survive your marriage, playing stupid becomes your best role. She's steaming, "I DON'T BELIEVE YOU LET ME WALK!!!"

"But, baby, you said you wanted to walk. I just wanted you to be happy and have your way, that's all."

Yeah, being stupid and bad lying—that about fills up your days at home when you're married. Women will force you to lie to them with questions like "Does Toni Braxton look good to you?" "No—too skinny!" No other woman looks good to you but your woman—that's the lie they want to believe, but even they don't believe it, as much as they would like it to be true. A man is under so much pressure when he sees a good-looking woman coming down the street. "Lord, don't let me look. I don't want trouble."

But your wife already saw this woman a half hour ago. She's got some super senses that put Superman to shame, and she's standing there all angry, just waiting for you to notice the woman. All you notice is how angry she is: "What's wrong with you?"

"Oh, you'll find out, Mister Nasty-Mind." The woman is striding right by you now and you're all turned in on yourself trying not to look, but it doesn't work, because your wife knows that in your heart, you want to look. "Go ahead and look, Mister Dog. You're just a *dog*, that's what's wrong with you."

The real pressure when you're married comes on the beach. Women don't wear bathing suits anymore. They're wearing dental floss and just pull it up.

One of those Floss Foxes comes swaying by. Once again, your wife makes you lie to her. "Is that what you want? I'm talking to you! Answer me, *Mister Dog*, is that what you want?"

"Oh, no. I didn't even see her until you pointed her out. Her butt's way too *small* for me, honey. I like the way *your* butt drags in the sand so nice. You leave that little trail so I can always find you. Come on, honey, write my name in the sand with your butt like you used to."

But I guess the thing that truly ruins the mystique of marriage is the bathroom. Once you've seen your woman use the bathroom, it's all over. See, when you're dating, women are sly and never let you be close to them when they go to the bathroom. If necessary they will hold it in for the whole date if they can't slip away to "fix their hair."

That's why we're so shocked when we marry and realize our wives go to the bathroom. Actually, I think many couples go into a kind of weird role reversal about the bathroom once they're married. Most men usually like to settle in for some quality time in the bathroom with newspapers, magazines, books, homework. That's where we thought we had guaranteed quiet to get some good thinking done. A man can sit in the bathroom for maybe nine or ten days. Suddenly, you find your wife has become all *open* about going. She's telling you, "Come right in." She's ready to hold court—I guess it's a strange show of affection, the first time you and she are both in the bathroom together and she wants to talk: "So, what do you want to do today?" Well, you don't want to *come right in.*

Here's an important tip for married men: Remember that a woman can go through a twenty-pack of toilet paper over the weekend. There'll be like five sheets left, and you'll never check till the last minute—too late! So keep your own stash. Otherwise, you'll end up like you were when you were single—running to the kitchen for the Bounty towels, pants around your ankles—but with a difference: She'll have invited people over and they'll be sitting there in your living room. All laughing at you.

Divorce: Show Me the Money!

"I'm tired of you squeezing the toothpaste all the way to the end."

"Well, I'm tired of you leaving your nasty socks all over the house."

"Yeah, well I'm tired of your mother calling at three in the morning."

"Yeah, well I'm tired of your family acting like our house is McDonald's."

Sounds pretty stupid, doesn't it? Nobody breaks up over such minor annoyances, do they? Sure—these days people shoot each other over less than that, and as nasty as most breakups are, I'm shocked that there aren't more "accidental" divorce-linked homicides. In fact, that's why I strongly recommend you do not keep a loaded gun on your premises, because if you do, just know that at some time during one of those really blood-boiling arguments the two of you are having there will come the moment when both of you are going to suddenly stop shouting and fling yourselves in the direction of whichever drawer or closet you've hidden that pistol away.

Hey, that's why I no longer keep silverware in my kitchen. It may not be classy, but I don't think the cops will ever discover my body lying in a pool of blood with a plastic knife sticking out of my pajamas, and my woman sobbing, "I couldn't take it anymore—it just drove me crazy how he smacked his lips when he chewed his Froot Loops."

Strange as it sounds, when you are in love with someone, *anger* can suddenly swell up in you that you never had in your life. It's intense, and after you've been together long enough, you both know just what to do to make each other's anger really explode. You don't waste time with the little insults, you go right for the jugular. Women who used to be sweet and shy and quiet learn how to make a face that would scare even Mike Tyson, staring right at their man and growling, "I'll *hurt* you right where you're standing. Tell me I won't!" Or worse, she'll be on the phone to her friends, "Girl, you better come get me. I'm going to hurt him," and they'll be egging her on, "You *go*, girl!"

So, it doesn't matter whether it's one big thing or just one too many of these kinds of fun arguments that help fill your happy days when you're a couple—the chances are that your breakup is probably coming, and it ain't going to be pretty! There is an old saying: "That which does not kill me only serves to make me stronger." Well, that doesn't apply to divorce. Divorce has so many ways to kill you: mentally, physically, spiritually, financially . . . Did I say financially? I think you get the picture. Did I mention financially?

One of the things that makes breaking up tougher today is that women have become tougher. You can't leave a woman like you used to. You used to leave a woman and she would just fall apart screaming and crying, "OH, I'LL KILL MYSELF!! OH, JESUS!!" While she was carrying on, you dog, you could just walk right past her: "I'm going out."

Not now. Your woman's been with you ten years and you've got four kids, and you, you fool, decide you've got to scratch your itch, and you strut in and announce, "Baby, I can't take this anymore. I've got to go."

"Go *where*? You mean you're going to walk around for a while and come back? I've been here ten years, too. And I've had a job. You're not going to walk out that door. If you go out that door, you're going out limping!"

The next day you'll see that brother hopping around on the one leg she didn't shatter with a baseball bat and he'll be mumbling to himself, "Yeah, *I* left."

It is easier to break up with somebody you've only been dating for a while—and this is true for a man or a woman—but it's still a lot harder than it should be. Why? The number one mistake people make is they don't follow the Parachute Rule: Jump early and keep your hand on the cord at all times.

You see, you've got to think of yourself as the pilot, the Sky King, of your relationship. When the needles on your instrument panel of love start moving into the red zone, you've got to reach for that parachute and, hey, you've got to Geronimo—jump out of that plane without thinking one more minute. Because just like on that plane, if you don't get out when you are still high enough above ground so your parachute can work, if you let that plane get too low to the ground before you jump out, you are going to get jacked-up when that parachute doesn't open right. Get out when there's plenty of altitude and you might even get to enjoy a little of the ride on the way down. Remember, you get to see more new prospects on the fields below from high above. When you bail out too low, all you're going to see and feel is ground and the pain comes a lot harder. In essence you get jacked twice.

Don't ignore those feelings that tell you it isn't working out. If the doctor told you you had some terrible disease that was operable, would you be fool enough to say, "Well, I'm not sure. I'm not feeling that bad all the time, let me give it a few more weeks before I let you save my life?"

Dating is like medication; there are "good" drugs and there are "BAD" drugs. A good drug (good date) is like aspirin, Tylenol, Novocain, it makes you feel better. Now bad drugs (bad date) are LSD, XTC, heroin, crack—they make you feel good for a short time, but after the rush is gone, what a crash! You know the bad drugs are hurting you but you keep going back to the pusher man (or woman) because you are strung out. The difference between drugs and dates is, there are rehab centers for the drug addict—there are no Betty Ford clinics for strung-out lovers. You have to go cold turkey.

I say, why put yourself through this? If by the third date it's not working out, you go, "Look, I had a wonderful time with you, or I thought I did, but I realized that it was mainly when you weren't there."

"What are you saying?"

"I'm saying that when you're actually next to me, it sucks."

I'm saying, "Just say *no*."

And don't go crazy trying to find some dignified, respectable way to break up—there is none. *Just do it!* (I love those Nike ads—maybe they should do a line of breakup shoes.) Look, we make dates by phone so why not just reach out and dump someone? That could be a new phone company slogan.

If you're really clever and quick, you can call when you know you'll get their answering machine—that way there's nobody embarrassed and there's no anger or shouting. If you think they're screening their calls, talk real fast and keep going even if they pick up—just pretend you don't hear them and hang up.

Now, I believe you can only dump by phone within the first five dates. After the fifth date you've got to break up face-to-face. But you still can apply the rules of dating and pull it off with style. Take him or her out to dinner at a great restaurant, sit him or her down and say, "Order anything you want, because this is the last meal I'm gonna be buying. Go ahead, eat some pie, get all big, it doesn't matter to me anymore. And here's a bus pass to get home because your riding days with me are over."

If you're on the receiving end, and you don't want to break up, please fight your instinct to try to salvage the relationship. Men, we are especially guilty of this. Because we are the ones who, after ten years of trouble, will drop our voices and ask, with more sincerity than we have ever shown before in the relationship, "Can I just talk to you for five minutes?" What makes us think we can fix a relationship with a five-minute speech? But we won't take no for an answer—she could be married with kids, have moved to another state to get away from you, and you'll still appear from the dark shadows of some building: "I want to talk to you for five minutes . . ."

Fellows, let it go! Even if you're a trial lawyer or a used-car salesman who is great at making headway out of "no way," you've got to let it go. Why do you even want to try? When you're a successful used-car salesman the car leaves the lot and you don't have to see it again. But if you've begged, it just can't last. Pretty soon they're going to say, "Man, that was a great speech, but I still hate you." Or worse yet, "We'll always be friends." *Aaaghhhhhhh!* I hate that friend speech.

Actually, when a woman breaks up she usually already has somebody else to go to. By the time she tells you she's leaving, she's got a new hookup. She's just planning to ease into that new hookup. She's dropping *you*, turkey, she's not going *cold turkey*. Why, the moment she decided you weren't working out she started checking out the room.

And it's always to go to a new and improved version, the BBD, I call it—the Bigger and Better Deal. She can't wait to drive by you at the bus stop in her new convertible Jag that her new doctor boyfriend gave her and see you. *Beep! Beep!* "Here's your bus pass back, you're gonna need it." That is cold-blooded.

When a man breaks up with a woman, he finds the first hoochie mama he can and can't wait to show up the old girlfriend.

"Look, I got somebody—"

Before you can stop her, your new hoochie mama slurs out with her gold tooth shining, "Dat's right!"

"Aw, I told you, keep your mouth shut and don't say anything. Just stand there." But your moment of triumph is busted.

For those couples who want to try to stay together, there is therapy. Therapy is tricky. Therapy usually favors the woman because women are used to talking about their feelings. Men aren't.

Women will gab at each other for fifty-seven hours, breaking down every emotional thing they're going through into nuances. A man will sit down with his buddy and his buddy will ask, "What's up with your wife?" The man will mumble, "Oh, man, she's *tripping.*" End of analysis.

Women love therapy sessions because they can't wait to tell on you. No question—they can outthink and outtalk you on the field of feelings. Women know how to get the therapist on their side. Their main goal is to get a professional to co-sign that you are a jerk.

When your woman has convinced you to go to therapy with her it usually comes at the point when so much hate has been spilling between the two of you your house looks like a toxic waste site. You begin wondering whether you ever were in love. So, you go to your first appointment with the therapist. There's the two of you, sitting and not looking at each other. You're feeling that really stupid kind of ornery so when the therapist just says, "Look at her," you snap, "No, I'm not looking at her," and you even cross your legs like a bratty little boy.

The therapist says, "I want you two to go away somewhere this weekend and write down five things that you like about each other."

"Five? Five! If I could write down five things I liked about her I wouldn't be here paying you all this money. How about just one thing? We need to put a stop to this nonsense and stop coming here real quick."

If the therapist irritates both of you, you can get some temporary zip back in your relationship if you both team up and fight with *her* and that at least gives you some fresh sport for your money. After all, you can fight with each other for free on your own time.

Most of the counselors are women, and most of them are not involved in a relationship of their own. Hah! Try asking your therapist about that. If she's not in a relationship, she'll never admit it. She'll turn it into a question. They turn everything into questions. She'll ask, "What are your feelings about my being in a relationship?"

"My feelings are that if you aren't in a relationship, you're the wrong person to tell me about my relationship."

Then she'll nail you for being hostile and your about-to-be ex will scream out, "See, he's hostile like this all the time."

Right there you'll be wishing you had one double-barreled shotgun, not to shoot them, but to turn both barrels on yourself. I don't think marriage therapy works.

Which leaves us with the Big D—*Divorce*. I've been in those jungles, I've fought those firefights, I'm carrying my scar tissue. I'm a veteran. I know whereof I speak.

When I was growing up, if you got divorced, it generally meant you had to move back home. You would rather be in a bad marriage for a hundred years than move back in to live with your parents at age thirty. These days, divorce is a whole lot more common. But that doesn't make it any easier really.

It should be easy. You should just be able to move on, maybe with a letter of resignation for divorce that you put on file when you get married. After all, if you can write your own stupid wedding vows, why can't you write your own letter to get yourself out of the marriage? If bad poetry can get you married, bad poetry should be able to spring you free:

> You were my sunshine
> Now you're my rain
> Turned out you were nothin'
> But a bad butt pain!
> Signed,
> Me

Of course, we can't just let it be this easy. No, we've got to trot out the lawyers. I cannot say it strongly enough, AVOID DIVORCE LAWYERS. As Spike Lee would say (or was it Malcolm X), "by any means necessary" keep away from lawyers—yours and hers. You can always tell the difference between couples who did their own divorces and those who used lawyers. The ones without lawyers brag about how they are better friends now than when they were married. As a matter of fact they probably even introduced their exes to their new mates, "I have someone great for you to meet . . ."

Now, the ones who used lawyers—well, that's a whole different scenario. They get on their knees each night and pray a special prayer, "Dear God, please let a semi-truck hit my wife/husband and please let me be there to see it so I can smack him/her right before he/she takes his/her last breath—Amen."

Sometimes I think that just before God threw Adam and Eve out of the Garden of Eden He looked ahead and said, "I've got to get these two a lawyer to help them work things out," and He took another bone from Adam and created the divorce lawyer. But God took that bone from Adam's *butt*—I'm not bitter, though.

Usually, the person making more money has to pay the attorneys. Great. That's the equivalent of me fighting Mike Tyson and having to pay for his trainer *and* my trainer. Now, even that wouldn't bother me so much if we got to settle this the only way I think is fair: I believe that the two people in the divorce should go into a ring, put on boxing gloves, and whoever comes out gets to keep all the stuff.

Only a form of life as low as the divorce lawyer could come up with an idea as twisted as "alimony." I don't understand alimony. The concept is you're supposed to provide for spouses to live in the manner they're accustomed to. The problem with that is they only pick the good years to be accustomed to. Hey, what about the years we had to catch the bus and do our wash at the Laundromat, when we were accustomed to coming home to find our electricity and phone cut off? Hey, boys and girls, can you say "selective amnesia"?

"Your Honor, how can I live on $200,000 a year? The children will starve."

Indeed, the dictionary tells us that alimony is a means of livelihood, of maintenance. *Maintenance?* Hah!

Now, I know what it means to do "maintenance" on a house. I pay the rent or the mortgage, I maintain the roof, the yard, the plumbing. But since when do you maintain a house that you no longer live in and no longer own? If I'm paying maintenance on my car it means I have the oil changed, I check the tires and make sure everything is running okay on a regular basis. I'm maintaining my car. I'm maintaining my car because I'M STILL DRIVING MY CAR. Once I am no longer driving that car my responsibility to that car is over. What if somebody stole your car and then sent you a bill for the oil change and a new transmission? You would say to that person, "You must be crazy—I'm not sending you a dime!" That's what I kept trying to tell my ex, but her lawyer wouldn't pass on the message. At least that's what my lawyer told me.

I'm not really against all alimony, just stupid alimony and especially unlimited alimony. I'm against *I-want-to-see-you-bleed-and-hope-you-never-have-anything alimony.* In California they compute your alimony based on some table the Wizard of Oz might as well have made up for all the sense it makes. You might spend $100 a month for the oil in your house. All of a sudden they look at their charts and the judge puts down $400 a month.

"But I never spent *that much* on the house."

"We don't care. These are the figures we came up with."

•   •   •

find it amazing that you have more rights in divorce than you do when you are married. If you are the chief (as they say in alimony) provider for the family, if you are the worst stingy tightwad, your significant other cannot take you to court. If your husband or wife won't give you enough money while you are married, I don't know of a court or agency in the land that will help you out and make them fork over more money to you. Only when you divorce this person—leave them—only then will somebody wake up and say, "Hey, we'd better get you some more money to live on properly."

I think every man or woman who gets slapped with alimony starts singing that old Johnny Taylor song at some point, "It's Cheaper to Keep Her (Him)."

Once it's final, divorce leaves you with some *crazy* feelings. I was guilty of driving by my old house when I no longer lived in it, just to look at it.

Most women, after their divorce, are smart—they usually go back for the education they might have missed, make new and better friends, pick up new hobbies; basically doing all those things they wanted to do before they got married.

Now men do just the opposite. They regress to about fifteen years old, when the world was new. They just look worse. A newly divorced man will rent (can't buy yet, wife had the good credit) a James Bond bachelor pad: 7,000 square feet but only one bedroom and half a bath (we don't need a sink—toilet and shower and we are cool), forgetting that he needs a place for his four kids to sleep—and occasionally wash up—when they come to visit. Then he rushes out and trades in the minivan (wife got the cool car) for a Corvette, once again forgetting that the kids might want to ride in the car with him when he goes to pick them up. The classic *jerk*! (Sorry, guys, had to side with the women on this one.)

Kids. Yes, divorce is toughest on them. I've got two, so I know, and nothing is more important to me in my life right now than to be real close to my son and daughter. That's one of the things I think is most unfair about divorce: It's usually assumed that the father is not an equally essential part of the parenting equation. Now your payments are important, and your potential earnings are important, but your attendance is not required. When I heard the judge grant me every other weekend, at first I thought, "My God! I'll never see them again." That's when I made my plans to kidnap my kids, move to Brazil, and become Pepi the clown. Again, this is one of those things where even if you've been a horrible, inattentive, uninvolved father while you are married, there's no punishment. But once you're divorced, even the best of fathers can be kept from his children.

If you have kids, after the divorce I recommend doing what we did, get two houses no more than thirty minutes apart. If you don't have kids, set up those houses a minimum of *30,000 miles* apart.

ey, enough of this negative energy. I think the people in New Orleans have the right idea when they celebrate death with a party. Since they say divorce is a lot like death (you mean I have to go through this twice or, if Shirley MacLaine is right, forever?), then why not let the good times roll?

That's right, celebrate your divorce. Yes, you can

turn that awkward, cold, formal, ugly situation into a ceremony celebrating your "un-marriage." You could even go all out and invite the same bunch of friends and relatives to join you for a "wedding in reverse." Your guests would gather and you would both march backward down the aisle of the church and stand at the altar where the same preacher or judge watches over you both reading your marriage vows *backward* or saying that stupid poetry you wrote together when you were so much in love (it will probably sound better read backward), somebody throws the bouquet back at the bride, and the little flower girl should *pick up* petals as you're walking. And of course, you should still have the party afterward. Everybody can bring you a matching gift to the one they brought originally—after all you're each going to need your own toaster and samovar now. If you're really ambitious, you can even go back to your original honeymoon hotel and try to get them to give you your money back. Good luck, you *go*, boy!

Done right, I think the "wedding in reverse" can be a useful celebration of your new life. After all, there is life after divorce, and it can be a pretty good one. And remember that you will love again, that there's a cover for every pot, that you will find that special someone to complete you.

Next time though, DON'T SHOW THEM THE MONEY!

That Weight Thing

Let's talk about building up, slimming down, bulking up, tearing up, ripping up, striating—there's a word for you—running down, pumping up, and all the other cute words that sell billions of dollars' worth of diet and muscle-building products every year: products that don't work. It's rare to find somebody who's happy with the way he's built. You're either too big or you're too small—there's no such thing as medium. We're in a constant state of toning down and toning up, of building up and cutting down.

Women, especially: There's not a woman in America who likes the way she looks. Try complimenting one: "You've got great legs"—"Oh, but you should see my *feet* . . ." "I love your eyes"—"Oh, but my elbows are all *ashy* . . ." Never happy.

Well, I'm going to help you with all that. The first

thing to know is that you're never too fat or too thin—
it's all in the people you've got hanging around. If
you're big, stick with folks who are bigger than you,
and they'll call you Slim. If you're skinny, go with
people who are scrawny and you'll feel bulked up. You
see that—I've just saved you from wasting hours and
thousands of dollars on the gym.

Now let's talk nutrition—how about Power Bars, Tiger's Milk, powdered protein, and this new thing that's
big now, the Zone? The Zone diet, you've got to eat
every two hours—yeah, like that's going to work. You
spend all that time in the Zone, you're going to lose
your job. No, I've learned the truth. After extensive
scientific research, I've discovered who the healthiest
and happiest people are: children on the playground.

I spent three years hanging out with kids—eating
what they eat and doing what they do—and I've
learned that fast food and candy are the mainstays of
life. If you think I'm lying, try taking a kid into a
health food store. It's like that scene in *The Omen*
where they take the devil child into a church. Beware!
Nothing good can come of it.

As for candy, the kind you eat is very important.
The top of the list is penny candy. Nowadays, it would
be called dollar candy. A dollar! Why, you couldn't
give a kid a dollar in the seventies. He would OD.
They'd find him in an alley somewhere, unconscious
and quivering, with Sugar Babies all around him on the
ground. "He killed himself with Sugar Babies," the
other kids would say, right before picking up whatever
was left. "Hey, it doesn't look like he needs that jawbreaker anymore."

Back then, candy was serious. A jawbreaker *would*

break your jaw. There was no gum in the middle, it was a rock with candy around it. You weren't supposed to get to the middle. It was so big you couldn't keep it in your mouth more than five seconds at a time or you would choke.

There was one candy you had to use in moderation, because it could string you out: Pixy Stix—Kool-Aid in a straw. In the playground, you'd go over to the Pixy bushes, where some brother would have himself set up with some of those giant, industrial-sized plastic Pixy Stix. "Here, my man, let me fix you up with a little taste of lemon-lime and have yourself a little grape while you're in the neighborhood." Then he would sprinkle some of that bright-colored sugar powder on your nasty playground hands and you couldn't lick it off fast enough, dirt and all. It tasted so good to you, you just did not care.

But for most of us, in a day spent scoring as much candy as we could, we always saved the best for last: that candy necklace. You wouldn't eat it until six o'clock. Your neck would have twelve different candy colors running down onto your shirt. The necklace would have bugs and crud sticking to it—but, never mind, you just popped those candy jewels into your mouth. We weren't worried about diseases then, so you'd tell your friend, "Go ahead, bite one off," and he would attack your neck like a vampire, grab ahold of some, and then that necklace, now full of his slobber, would snap right back tight to your neck.

Aaah, but once you hit thirty, the body gets cruel. When you're fifteen, you don't need a diet. You can eat a bag of Oreos and lose five pounds. You hit thirty, though, and you just *walk* by a cookie store and *smell* some cookies, and *bam!!*—fat just jumps onto your body. You cry, "God, I didn't eat one of those cookies. I swear! I was just looking!"

It doesn't matter, because when it comes to food, once you're thirty and that Ol' Devil Metabolism kicks in, there is no God.

Or if there is a Food God, it's bound to be a woman because women take their dieting so much more seriously than men. Women go on that "I'm Gonna Lose 20 Pounds by Next Wednesday" Diet. "Girl, I'm gonna wear this next week." You've been fat for twenty-seven years and suddenly you got that twenty-year high school reunion coming up and you're desperate. "I can't go like this!" Why not? You were fat all through high school, so nobody's expecting you to be slimmer now.

Women come up with some really weird weight loss systems I've never heard of before. "See, what I'm doing is drinking a bottle of water—it's got to be ice-cold water—and then eating a bit of a Snickers bar. It's the Snickers Diet. That chocolate keeps me going!"

Women get violent when they go on diets. A woman goes on a diet and she asks you to help her, but she's lying. She says, "No, baby, I want you to help me."

"Yeah, right. I'll help you—go to McDonald's and get you another sandwich . . . I'm not gonna stop you. I fell for that last time. When you want your sandwiches, *you're* gonna eat some sandwiches! Hey, I been there, sister. Trust me, it's not a pretty sight to see."

I really like those women who go on a Slim Fast diet and keep eating, like Slim Fast is going to just vacuum up that sandwich. They drink some Slim Fast and gulp down a double-wide, extra-greasy helping of ribs, "Girl, I'm on Slim Fast"—like it's some secret acid that's going to eat up all the food in their stomach and make it all just disappear!

But to me, the silliest diet I ever tried was Nutri System, where you follow their meal plans and buy their food packages. In 1989 I looked in the mirror and for the first time I yelled, "Hey, you've gained some weight!" So, I went to Nutri System. You know why you lose weight on Nutri System? 'Cause you're broke. You can't buy any more food on your own because it cost so much to get on Nutri System. People go, "You look good!"

You say, "Oh, I *want* to eat, I just don't have any money." I would be hanging out at McDonald's, tapping on the window after hours, "Don't throw out those fries—I'm on Nutri System. Please, bring them over here!"

I know some men who got dragged onto Nutri System by their women. A man will grumble, "I don't need Nutri System. I got my own system right here for eating. It's called my belly."

"Aw, baby, please, join with me. Please." When you're with somebody you've got to do that, but you just *know* he's got sandwiches hidden underneath the mattress that he's sneaking while she's asleep.

She goes, "How come you're never hungry on Nutri System?"

He's brushing crumbs from his pajamas. "Aw, baby, it just fills me up, what can I say?"

My first day at Nutri System, I spent all my money,

and the Nutri System lady gave me a bag. I said, "Where's the rest of my groceries?"

She said, "This is your meal plan for the week."

"No," I said. "You see, I'm gonna eat that in the car. That bag's not gonna make it home. I thought this was my snack while you pack the rest of my stuff up."

"These meals will fill you up."

"Oh, these will fill me up?" I dug some packages out of the bag. I swallowed. "There, I already ate Monday and Tuesday and I'm still hungry."

"Sinbad, if you get hungry, just eat a Nutri Chip."

"A chip? Let me get this straight. If I get hungry, I should open up the bag of Nutri Chips, pull out one chip—one chip—and close the bag back up? If I could do that I wouldn't be here at Nutri System! That's my problem. Once I open up that bag, sister, it's a meal, and anything that's near the bag is fair game, too."

Then they had that Nutri System chocolate spray. If you crave a chocolate bar they say you're supposed to spray the chocolate spray at yourself. People thought I was a crack addict I was sniffing so much chocolate spray. I was a full bottle a day habit. I was hanging out in the Nutri System parking lot, "Pssst! You got some of that chocolate spray?" I was *strung out* on chocolate spray. I had to go to Betty Ford for chocolate spray.

No question, though, the all-time worst experience I ever went through for losing weight was when I tried to lose weight the "natural herbal way." You know, that's where you cleanse your colon—I mean they *clean* your colon out, make your colon spic and span.

It started when I met this brother in a turban, so I thought he was legit. "Sinbad, my brother, you've been eating all that bad food for the last thirty-six years, and your colon is *impacted* with waste. We're going to break that up."

I said, "We better leave that alone. Let's just stop any new waste from coming in and leave that old waste alone."

I'm going to tell you something right now. If you're going to cleanse your colon, you better quit your job and go out into the woods somewhere. You cannot cleanse your colon while you're around people. You'll be slim, but you'll be funky. "Slim and Funky," that's what they're going to call you. "Hey, Slim, you're lookin' good . . . No! Stay over there, Slim! Don't come over here by me, please!"

You see, when you cleanse your colon, like when I was taking these herbs, you get *unnatural* gas.

Usually, you can stop your gas. That's why you have a butt muscle. That's your butt muscle's only job—to stop gas. Your butt will operate on its own. If something's about to slip out past you, your butt muscle says, "It's . . . all right . . . go on . . . I've got it contained."

When you get gas, what is the first thing you do? Tighten up! Now, when you tighten up, you can't move, you can't breathe, your body's shut down for about four seconds, but your mind doesn't know it. You think you're still moving, so you look like you're having a momentary seizure, but it works.

But, man, when I went on those natural herbs—the gas just came *sneaking* out. In my mind, I'm going, "Oh, they're not that bad." I looked behind me and trees were falling down, buildings were crumbling, and people behind were gasping for air, shouting, "Sinbaaaad . . . please stop . . . I can't see . . .

What's wrong with you, man? . . . Is something *dying* inside of you?"

So, my advice is, the next time you go on that special diet and you're tempted to cheat, think of my colon-cleansing program. I guarantee you'll put that sandwich back!

You're the Reason I'm Not Cool Anymore

This chapter is dedicated to the children of the world everywhere.

There's a country music song title that always makes me laugh: "You're the Reason Our Kids Are Ugly." Someday I may record my song to my kids: "You're the Reason I'm Not Cool Anymore."

That's right, for all you kids reading this book, your parents used to be cool. But don't feel bad, we also did it to our parents. It is just a law of nature—kids come, cool goes. Simple as that.

We still want kids, though pregnancy is tough on everyone, especially the man. That's right, I said especially the man. No one ever talks about how pregnancy and fatherhood affect us. Well—since this is my book and women already have 3 million books written for them—I'm telling our story. Who knows, women, you might even learn something, heaven forbid.

Let's get rid of some of these kid myths:

MYTH #1: Only a woman can know the pain of birth.

WRONG! We do know that pain. Not in the same sense as you do, but we feel it also. We feel it when the hospital hands us the bill for the doctor and all those other people in the room.

I started my Lamaze breathing on just the anesthesiologist's bill. $3,000, *for what?* Ladies, you keep talking about the pain, well, if you could hang in there just a little longer we could save those dollars.

Heck, what was the Lamaze class for? A chance to make us look stupid? My mother kept saying, "Boy, you are wasting your money." But I believed in all that natural, underwater, no trauma, bring-the-baby-gently-into-the-world stuff. I thought that Lamaze was going to work. My wife and I were the best breathers in the class, we have an award to prove it, "Couple Most Likely to Give Natural Birth."

Boy, that *breathing* didn't last long when the real deal came. I started breathing in my wife's face and saying all those cool Lamaze things, "Come on, honey, breathe. You can do it. Only eighteen more hours, hang in there."

She had this strange look on her face. I thought it was bliss, but it was more like pissed. She started whispering to me and I couldn't hear her, so I had to get close. Men, I learned something that day: Don't get within striking distance of your woman in the delivery room. They want to kill you. She pulled me by my eye —I didn't even know you could grab an eyeball. And she shouted in my ear, "If you don't quit breathing that funky breath in my face and get me some drugs quick, I am going to pull out this eye and throw it down the hall!" To this day I am looking for that Lamaze teacher so I can grab her eyeball and get my money back.

Now, we were ready for my second child. As a matter of fact, we were the best-dressed couple in the maternity ward that night. We were at the American Music Awards the night she went into labor. Michael Jackson, who was her favorite performer in the whole world, was onstage singing "Billie Jean." She started squeezing my hand real tight, I thought she was excited by the performance. WRONG AGAIN! She was going into labor. I could tell because her eyes were crossed, and she is not normally cockeyed. I told her that we should head to the hospital. She looked at me, at least I think she was looking at me, and told me if I tried to make her leave before Michael was done she was going to take the show program and stuff it through my navel, or something to that effect. I didn't really hear her—I was too busy trying to figure out who she was talking to.

When Michael got through we had to make a mad dash for the hospital. My brother Mark was also at the show, so he went with us. We were looking too good. When we got to the hospital, everyone was calm, nurses were saying how good we looked. We said thank you. It never hurts to be polite to people about to reach up inside you.

I had already made my connection with the drug

man before I got to the hospital. I had an anesthesiologist on call (I was *the man* that night). We didn't take one Lamaze breath on this trip—heck, we didn't even bother to take the class for the second child.

By the time I finished filling out the forms, she was higher than a kite, I mean *relaxed.* Men, drugs will make your woman happier. We had a nice conversation going the whole time, and her hair didn't even get messed up. I saved about a $200 beautician bill there alone. Because usually a black woman's hair, if you use the Lamaze technique, will revert back to its natural African state. I mean, *1661* A.D. There is no relaxer that can save that hair. You have to let it fall out and start all over. A lot of men thought their wife had naturally "good" hair until that first baby. The truth will come out.

Now, when our second child, Royce, was born, I was ready for how the baby was going to look, but when our first child, Paige, was born, I was not prepared for what I was about to see. This takes us to:

MYTH #2: All babies are beautiful.

Oh heck, no! I couldn't believe what I was seeing. On TV, babies are born all cute, with tennis shoes on and a big smile showing some teeth. Well, in real life they come out with these long banana heads—I thought I had a conehead for a child. I thought my child was going to have to wear a sock on her head for the rest of her life so she could fit in with the other kids. Now, my wife wasn't worried. You have to remember that mothers are kind of high, so they don't really know what they are seeing yet. Maybe fathers should take some drugs too, so we have time to acclimate ourselves to the "long-head sucker" (I was trying to think of a cool nickname before the other kids did).

Mothers love to show those ugly Polaroid pictures of the child at one hour old. Who takes those pictures anyway? I would have noticed a camera crew in there. They must come out with the baby. I'm just glad they are free. They should be, they made my child look like a pit bull. Now I know where the *Enquirer* gets those weird alien pictures.

Now, when we get the child home comes:

MYTH #3: "My child is special."

Parents start lying about their child's abilities right away. Nothing worse than being at the Discovery Zone on a Saturday listening to the mothers: "Three days old —my baby's walking! Look." You look over and this child is wearing those ugly white orthopedic shoes. Please, get real, that kid isn't special, a Jell-O pudding pop could stand up in those hard white shoes. "Oh yeah? My child's a genius; he's two and in college."

Parents lie to themselves and, worse, to their kids. The biggest lie they tell is: "My child can do anything. He is perfect. She is special."

It's time for us to start being honest. Sure, your child is special, but don't force people to have to lie to you. "Uh, her voice is so *different*." No—the child can't sing! And don't tell your funny-looking, big-eared child, "You'll grow into those ears." Tell it like it is: "Your ears are gigantic. Unless you learn how to jump like Michael Jordan you're going to have to wear a cap for the rest of your life."

The child whose parents recognize his defects will grow up well-adjusted. But there are those kids out there who are not ever going to be normal. I'm talking Jeffrey Dahmer, Charles Manson kind of kids. Yes, they were kids once just like everybody else—well, maybe not like everybody else. Take Dahmer, for instance. At some point his parents had to realize that all of his pets were missing and the kid was gaining weight. Now, the father knew. Fathers are brutally honest. "Lucille, you know that boy ate the dog. Yes, he did. I heard the dog barking, then I saw Jeffrey with a sandwich. And we haven't been grocery shopping in weeks. I'm telling you, he ate the dog. And I don't like the way he has been looking at me lately. Lucille, you better watch your back around that boy."

Mothers will defend their children to the end. Even when they caught Dahmer, Mom was protective: "Jeffrey always had a healthy appetite, who would have known that he was . . ."

MYTH #4: "I love all my children equally."

Yeah, right! That's a lie! Six kids, six different personalities—come on, no way you can treat them all the same. I've found that my favorite kids are the ones best at kissing my bootie. Not that they are smarter or stronger, they just do what I say without asking a single question. I try to avoid the ones that act like they are auditioning for the movie *Children of the Corn.* You know the type: too good with weapons, sleep with their eyes open, and believe Satan gets a bad rap.

MYTH #5: Similac is milk.

Have you ever had a baby regurgitate some fresh Similac on your clothes? It is like acid rain burning your flesh. You have to rip those clothes off your body before you peel. Similac would kill the average adult. Only a baby can handle something so toxic. Why do you think baby bowel movements smell so bad? It doesn't make any physiological sense for something that small to smell that bad. If you leave a bottle with Similac in it out in the sun for two hours, you will have bread. It's more than a drink, it's a sandwich.

But there are many good uses for Similac. If you are stuck on a deserted island and a case of Similac floats up on the shore, use it to start fires. Just pour it on some wood and back up and watch the fireworks. If you are hanging some wallpaper in your house and you run out of glue, take the bottle out of the baby's mouth and continue on with your work. The baby can help by licking the wall. Now you have a family project. Lord knows, we need more quality time with our families. More family time like this, and of course a lot of Similac, might have saved young Dahmer from a life of snacking.

MYTH #6: You will be able to help your children with their homework.

Let's face it, by the second grade you can no longer do the math. We didn't have that stuff in college. It is truly a shame when your seven-year-old son says, "Daddy, will you check my math?" and you have to lie and say, "I trust you, son."

I blame the schools. We are pushing our kids way too hard. My daughter's homework bag is heavier than the computer I take to work. She weighs sixty pounds, the bag weighs twenty—that's how kids get exercise today. We weren't allowed to take books home till junior high; I used to beg my teachers to let me carry out a book, homework seemed that cool to me. They would shake their heads, "Oh, no. That kind of heavy lifting will stunt your growth."

I'm afraid my daughter's sleeve inseam will be about forty inches from being stretched by the weight of that bag. Maybe that wouldn't be too bad, though, because then I wouldn't have to worry about her getting dates. Boys don't date girls with Stretch Armstrong arms.

Right now I am taking remedial math so I can help my son make it to the third grade. I have already failed my sixth-grade daughter. I lost her around the fourth grade.

I mean, that homework is tough! All our children would be flunking if we did their homework for them. I don't care if you're a college professor, a Ph.D., a doctor, a lawyer—by the fifth grade you just can't help them anymore. They could be lying to me for all I know. I just nod my head a lot when we talk about their homework. Folks go to night school to try to keep up, but it's hopeless, man—by a certain point, you outlive your usefulness as parents.

You can't even tell them anything about life. They've been dating for years without telling you. Besides, you still get shook up when discussing the opposite sex. They're making you recycle and they check up, so you have to be slick: "I stuck a dirty piece of tinfoil and a wet magazine in the organic bag—so sue me." All they eat is cookies and peanut butter and they can justify it by saying, "Meat is murder." I wish we had had animal rights when I was growing up. Kids today have even justified being funky because they say the deodorant spray is destroying the ozone layer. I say, "You build up enough funk on this planet and you will blow the ozone layer away."

"Not scientific, Dad." You can't win anymore.

When your kids reach this stage, you've got to face it—they just don't need you anymore. Oh, they still need your car—they are not worried about gasoline and the ozone layer, at least not on the weekend—and they have no guilt about the $2,000 for their class trip to the Bahamas, where you've never been. So who are you to say it won't be educational?

One thing hasn't changed, though. Even with all this worrying about college in third grade, a kid still better not get straight A's. It was like that even back when I was in school. I thought Square, Punk, and Sissy were my first, middle, and last names. Kids made me knee-walk home in the snow, all the while smacking me upside the head with drumsticks. The insulting part was, they were *my* drumsticks. I quit playing drums for two years after that. I'd have my friend standing by every day at lunchtime to get me out of my locker that they (the eighteen-year-old ninth graders that the Board of Education thought should get a second chance at life—thanks a lot) would lock me up in every day.

Today it's no better: You get beat up if you don't hide your brain. Kids lying in wait for you: "Come here, boy. Give me that report card. Uh-huh—what's up with these A's?"

"Those aren't mine, man. Somebody switched 'em— you know I'm down with y'all; you know I'm straight-up stupid. What could I do with an A—get a job? Come on, in five or six years I want to be flunked out of school and unemployed, just like you."

And it's hard to explain it to your parents: "How come you got beat up, son?"

"It's my grades, Mama. I got to flunk something. I can't take these beatings every day."

MYTH #7: You can still keep your cool car.

Way wrong. Did you read Myth #5? You think Similac messes up clothes, wait until it hits your new Corinthian leather upholstery. You might as well have gotten the standard cloth material. It can be replaced easier. As a matter of fact, when you have kids, just order everything standard on the car—no fancy stereo, power windows, sunroof, etc. The kids are going to kill all of that stuff. Take an ordinary cookie: In the hands of a kid it becomes a sugar hand grenade. One bite and *boom*—a cookie, splattered all over the car! Then you have to take the car into the shop because chocolate chips are clogging the carburetor. And all kids have jelly hands, even when there is no jelly to be found within twenty miles of your car. The jelly just oozes out of their hands and smears up your windows, until you almost crash the car trying to clean it off with Windex so you can see the other cars before you hit them. And don't even think that you can sneak food into the car without the kids knowing—they can sniff it out. Besides, you'll just frustrate yourself trying to sneak in bites while the kids aren't looking.

Just driving around also changes; all your landmarks are kid related now. You don't even think, "There's the pool hall, check out the cool suit in DJ's window, there's the park where I soul-kissed Yvonne under that big oak tree—that girl was fine—heard she had two kids and gained 500 pounds. Those must be some big kids." No, the streets don't have names anymore: Now it's "Go past the Discovery Zone and turn right at Gymboree, then take a left at the Chuckie Cheese . . ."

I am combining the next two myths because one always seems to follow the other:

MYTH #8: Kids can't just disappear into thin air!

and

MYTH #9: Kids are indestructible.

Here's the connection. Usually a kid who has disappeared from you doesn't show back up until he has jacked himself up doing only God knows what.

Yes, kids will mess you up—and they love doing it. Losing a child and having to take him to the emergency room—those are your worst parents' nightmares. So when you're shopping in a huge mall, your child will hide out in a rack of coats, just to see you freak out. While you are running around shouting out your child's name, losing your mind, he is hiding right next to you in a rack of clothes, cracking up at the show you are putting on. The first time this happens to you, you don't know what to do. You start off cool, whispering the kid's name: "*Psst*, Mark. Mark. Where are you, honey?" You try to maintain a friendly tone so everyone else thinks everything is fine. You have a smile on your face, knowing full well that when you find this kid he might as well give his soul to Jesus because his butt belongs to you. But after two minutes you're getting really worried. You start asking strangers, "Have you seen a little high-yellow black kid around here anywhere? I just looked away for a minute and he disappeared." You start defending yourself to people because you notice them staring and whispering, "What kind of parent loses a child? If you don't have time for them you just shouldn't have them." Don't even bother defending yourself—the childless experts are already calling the police and social services on you. People without kids always think they know the best way to raise children. These are the same people who end up writing books on child-rearing, like *Raising the Rambunctious Child* by Dr. I-Don't-Have-a-Child-but-I-Have-Some-Nieces-and-Nephews.

Thank God other parents understand and shoo the childless critics away. Then they help you out, as you will yourself do one day for some other new parent: "Honey, have you checked the coatracks?" Sure enough: BUSTED! You thank these wise sages, but they are not yet finished. They offer you a belt with which you can beat your child. "Do it now, before the kid thinks this is funny." It is like when Yoda gave Luke Skywalker his Jedi lightsaber—"*May the force be with you.*"

But you soon learn the coatrack scam is the easy one. Kids are just warming up with that one. I believe kids have the ability to dematerialize altogether. They can do it for the simple reason that they believe they can. I used to be able to do it myself, then I grew up and lost faith. It has something to do with getting a job. A lot of things change after entering the work force, but that's another book, *The Infantile Executive.*

One time my daughter, Paige, scared me half to death. I was home babysitting and she just disappeared. I was searching all over the house for about two hours. The worst thing that can happen to a man is to have his wife come home and he has lost the child. "How did everything go?"

"Great, we're playing hide-and-seek and she's winning."

You can't fool a mother, though. She knows you lost the child. "I knew something like this was going to happen. I should have taken her with me. You were on your computer, weren't you?" I hate when they are right. "No!" (lying through my teeth and sweating profusely).

We both start looking in and outside the house, all the while I am being reminded how irresponsible I am. Women have the gift of being able to search and talk about you at the same time without losing focus. She asks if I have looked in the closet, like I was too stupid to think of that. I tell her, "I checked *every* room five times, and where I come from the closet is considered a room." Lame, but I needed a victory.

Well, lo and behold, what should happen when my wife opens the closet door? *Ta-da*—there is Paige. Now, I was not lying, I *had* checked that closet five times. All I could do was assume the bad-husband pose—head down looking at my feet and mumbling,

"Did too check the closet, did too check the closet, did too check the closet." Meanwhile, Paige is acting strange. You know, that I-am-about-to-get-a-spanking-because-I-did-something-stupid look. She is breathing through her mouth and having a hard time of it. So I step forward with the daddy move, "What's wrong, baby?"

"Nothing"—the universal kid answer. I take a closer look and realize her nose is compacted with something. I ask her what is in her nose.

"Raisins."

"How many, Paige?"

"This whole box."

My child had jammed seventy-five raisins up her nose. I mean, jammed them so tight she couldn't breathe but wouldn't let on, afraid I'd be mad. Just sitting on a raisin box, trying to act cool. My wife, trying to be Marcus Welby, M.D., pulls a bobby pin out of her hair and says, "This'll get them out."

"No way—we're going to the hospital. Who knows what raisins can do to you? Maybe they can get into your brain!" So I grab Paige and run her to the hospital. Next time I will use the car. I guess you could say I panicked.

But in the emergency room, I felt stupid. Other kids were there with serious accidents—hit by cars, stuff fell on them, hands all burned up; just terrible—and I'm sitting there beside a child with raisins up her nose. My wife's brought the box; I'm arguing with her: "Like they care if it's a California raisin? A golden raisin? They got different ways to take them out?"

"Maybe they do, you don't know."

Nobody did. "Hmm," said the doctor. "I'd like to

check this with a colleague . . ." What, like one of y'all took a class—"Foodstuffs in the Nose"? Like there's a specialist to call?

Finally they find a way to remove the raisins—they use a bobby pin. Proven wrong twice in one day, I'm not able to go home for a while. I couldn't handle the "I told you so" and "Maybe you'll listen to me next time" soliloquies. Oh, Paige was fine. Man, but for a while she had me sweating.

Another terrifying situation is when a child does something that almost gets him killed. You can tell it by the way he comes home. He runs in the house, all out of breath and shaking, comes over to you and, in a hoarse, squeaky voice, says: "I just love you so much. I'm never going back outside!"

Sure enough, they almost killed themselves. And you don't want to know the truth. You couldn't handle it. I know, because I was the king of doing death-defying dumb stuff. My favorite one was hiding in bushes and waiting for a car to come by so we could jump out in front of it and make it squeal all its tires trying to stop. Sometimes you won—and *one* time you didn't. That's what made it a good game! You would be surprised how many kids I got to join me in this game. I was that ringleader parents always warn their kids about. I lost a lot of friends that summer.

MYTH #10: Spanking is the only way.

First of all, I am not an advocate of *time-outs*. One day they are going to find out some kid came up with that idea. Great con.

I do believe in the theory "Spare the rod and spoil

the child." I just don't believe in doing time after my kid calls the police on me. But there are *alternative* methods you can use. You are just going to have to be creative and experiment to find out what works on your child. I found some techniques that work for me.

For example, when kids get about four to six years old, they start to steal. Not because they're criminals, at least not yet. It's as simple as, you said no and they wanted the stuff. The kid will walk out of the store and there's eight candy bars under his shirt. "Where did you get that candy?"

"Uh, from Mommy."

"Your mom and I have been divorced for three years now."

"Oh yeah, I forgot."

So you do the most embarrassing thing you can do to a child, you make the child go back in the store and tell the store manager that he stole some candy and that he is sorry and wants to pay for it. I would rather have my father beat me with a rubber hose while I'm buck naked and lying on 100-degree asphalt in the parking lot than face the store manager. Now I will be branded as "that thieving child" for the rest of my life. To this day, whenever I go into that Kroger's store back home, that now seventy-five-year-old man follows me around, calling out, "You thieving child." It is embarrassing.

The worst part was coming out of the store and having to stand in the crowded parking lot listening to my dad lecture about the evils of stealing. "Do you want to go to jail, huh? You want to be a criminal, is that what you want?" Then he would surprise me with the second half of the speech. (Remember, my dad's a preacher, so a speech could last as long as a ballgame—and I'm talking baseball.) "Next time you want to steal, steal something worthwhile, something I can use. Go and get us some pants, 36 waist."

After all that talking, I still might have gotten a whupping when I got home. I try not to whip my kids. I have come up with my own technique. I call it the *duct tape* way to peace and harmony with your child. If a kid acts up, duct tape them to the floor right where they are putting on a show. Nothing like being taped to a moving escalator to change a child's attitude. Just don't let the childless police see you. It even works with potty training. Kid doesn't want to stay on the pot, strap their butt in. Something about walking around with a potty strapped to your hiney that makes a kid want to go, bad. Crude, but effective—not to mention economical. You can buy four miles of duct tape for $5 at your warehouse club.

Whenever you see one of those families in the mall and the kids are behaving ("Johnny, put that down." "Okay, Mommy.") and you wonder how they do it—DUCT TAPE. If you check that mother's purse I guarantee there will be a roll or two of it in there.

MYTH #11: The family that plays together, stays together.

Sure, I love my kids and I know they love me. But you can get too much of a good thing. It's all right for a family to take breaks from each other every now and then.

I love being a father. I was shocked at how good a father I became—*bam!*—right from day one. Part of the reason is the cool stuff kids have now. Today they make it easier to be a parent. They have these kiddie expos where you can get all the coolest equipment. Baby seats used to weigh 200 pounds, now they're 16 ounces, made of titanium; they have whole cars with no backseat, just a built-in playpen with a VCR and tape deck—rubber, so they can chew them—soundproof, so Raffi can't get into grown-ups' brains; even kiddie beepers—they can't talk but they can wake you up: "Goo, goo, goo . . ." From the jump, I was a high-tech daddy. I had this cool mountain backpack to carry my kids in. I was able to take my kids with me everywhere. The only drawback to the backpack is the babies pour that acidic Similac down your neck. At least I have no more back hair.

As the kids grow up, they kind of get into their own thing. And you treasure your "quiet time" also. My son, Royce, loves playing by himself. Give him a rubber band or a paper clip and he's got an army. One time he was having fun in his make-believe world, and I thought, "Hey, let me go play with my son." I grabbed one of his paper clips and started acting crazy with him, and he just quit. He looked up at me and said, "Daddy, I kind of like playing by myself," then he gave me that big fake *kid smile.* So I left the room and shut the door. Quality time—about three minutes' worth. But it's cool.

The worst things are those forced "we're going to eat dinner as a family" affairs. Everybody's supposed to sit down and talk. Good theory. In actuality, it is torture. With a big family, you'd have to set up that pull-apart table—pinch your hands!—the double-leafer, with two extra boards, too long for the room, so someone's sitting out in the hall. Then it's mass confusion as you fight for the food, trying to get done before your mama asks you something embarrassing or your brothers think up something to tattle about.

I'd never do that to my kids, man. As a child, all I wanted was to eat in peace, off a tray, alone in my room. Not much has changed, except I have a TV in my room now.

At family dinners there was okra, beans with strings in them, and all the other foods kids hate. The food I hated the most was the pieces of bread at the ends of the loaf—I called it the *bootie bread.* No way would I eat that bootie bread. I couldn't even stand to have it on my plate. My mother would scold me, talking about the poor kids in Third World countries who had no food. "Like you've seen them," I'd say. "If you can name me one, I'll eat this." She couldn't—and I didn't. Although I did get a whupping for getting smart.

I believe—and science is going to prove—that all children should eat is sugar. You can see it for yourself: Turn him loose in the house and watch a child's sense of smell take him straight to the Snickers and Butterfingers or to the stale half donut you forgot to throw away. "Daddy! Candy!" That's why cereal is the breakfast—and lunch and dinner—of champions for children. And I don't mean cardboard cereal like Cheerios, I mean the real deal, like Apple Jacks and Frosted Flakes. Tony the Tiger was good to us. Forget about milk—fruit juice, Hawaiian Punch, or even soda pop can do the job better, which is to pack your kids full of the sugar they crave. It's instinct—they'll go for the Crunch Punch (Hawaiian Punch poured over Captain Crunch) over the bran muffin. Don't try to fight it.

There's no way you can win. And they can fix cereal themselves, so you can sleep in—that's why I made sure my kids got hooked.

Remember, not all quality time is time spent together; some of the best quality is time spent apart. "Absence makes the heart grow fonder" doesn't just apply to lovers.

MYTH #12: Don't worry, they'll forget.

Anything you say or promise a kid will be remembered until the day you die. They will be standing over your grave, "But you promised me . . ." A lot of parents don't realize, say, that a Christmas list is not just a list of items to a kid, but a binding contract to be fulfilled. Most of the insecure adults you meet today are that way because their parents didn't take the list seriously enough.

One Christmas I asked for a horse. I already thought I was the Lone Ranger, with my toy gun and my mask, the cuff of a sock with two eyes cut out. Six or seven years old—all I wanted was a horse, so I just knew Santa had brought me one.

Early Christmas morning I snuck downstairs—no horse in the living room or kitchen. Then I realized, "Of course! A horse can't be inside." It was freezing out, snowing, but I ran to check the yard and the garage. No horse.

Then Mama came to the door. "Get in here! Out in your pajamas and slippers—you're going to catch your death of cold!"

"Mama, Mama, the horse is loose!"

"What? Come in!"

"Someone took him!"

"Took who?"

"My horse from Santa Claus. We got to find him."

"Son"—she's on the porch now—"Santa didn't bring you a horse."

I'm like, "How do you know? Who told you?"

She goes, "Santa has the sense to know we could never keep a horse in the yard."

"There's that big field behind it."

"That's not our field."

"Well, I could just keep him tied up . . ."

"Listen to me, child, there is no horse. You didn't get one."

I was just crushed. I couldn't believe it. It hurt me for years.

When I finally did get up on a horse for the first time, it was like a scene from a movie or a comic book —like, mythical. I was thirteen years old, at camp, I didn't have many friends. Since I was known as the kid who blew up frogs with firecrackers, their parents didn't want me around. Walking back alone from swimming, I heard hoofbeats coming up fast and a man yelling, "Get off the path, boy. Get out of the way." I turned around and there was this huge black stallion behind me; his hide was shiny, and riding him was a great big black man. A black cowboy! I looked so shocked that he had to stop. "Whatchu looking at, never seen a man on a horse before?"

"Not a black man—can I ride with you? Can you teach me?" He reached down and grabbed me up behind him, and we rode back to the stable he owned, down the road from my camp.

"You want to learn?" he said. "First you have to

respect the animal, so brush him down and clean out his stall." I was there cleaning till the sun went down, and then I got ready to walk back.

"Whoa, son," he said. "Did you lose heart? You don't think you can learn to ride when it's dark out?" I sat up there on the horse all by myself—cool, but scary —while the guy showed me the moves; and then I came back every day.

I kept the riding a secret until, one day, the cowboy was leading some riders down the trail—kids all sitting on the ground, watching the horses go by—and he called out: "Want to run a horse back to the stable for me?"

"Who, me?" I said.

"Are you deaf, boy? Yes, you." But I was already running, and then—*phoom!*—I jumped onto that saddle. Galloped away like a pro.

It was the greatest moment of my life, man—sitting up on that horse, looking down at all those kids who thought I was crazy, I felt so special, almost powerful. I think the cowboy knew what he was doing for me, making me stand out like that in front of the rest of the kids. If I hadn't been crazy, I never would have asked for the ride, never would have spent my days cleaning the man's stalls, never would have learned.

But try telling your kids that story: "So, children, the moral is, just be yourself. In oddness lies your strength. Never mind what people think. You don't have to be Mr. Popularity . . ."

"Oh yes I do, oh yes I do—Daddy, you're so ignorant."

Save your breath!

Pop-Tart Time

In the old days, you got up at three o'clock in the morning to start preheating the oven to 350°; by five, you could put in the Pop-Tarts, and two and a half, three hours later, they'd be brown and ready to eat. Waiting was part of life—you just accepted it. But the good thing was that you got to know your brothers and sisters, waiting two or three hours for the Pop-Tarts to brown—talking about your dreams, what kind of car you were going to have. But now you stick a muffin in the microwave, push the button, and—*bam*—you start peeking in the door and stomping around the kitchen: "Hurry up!" Those sixty seconds drive you crazy. Sixty seconds is not enough time to get to know your wife— that's why there's so much divorce now. What we need is more *Pop-Tart* time.

We've all got the *need to speed*. Everything's got to

be this minute. True, technology is partly to blame, but our own self-importance has a lot to do with it.

How about call waiting: It used to be that when you tried to call Grandma at night and the line was busy, you'd take a ride over to her house to make sure she was okay and that nothing had happened to her. Now you get a busy signal and slam down the phone: "How could you not have call waiting?" You're screaming, "Get off that phone! Hang up!" like she can hear you. But like my grandmother used to say, "I've got call waiting. You call and the line is busy, you wait till I get through."

Ah, speed! Speed is addictive. Once you get used to it, you've got to have more of it. For example, say you used to ride the bus to work, but one time somebody gives you a ride. Now the bus is too slow. And when you buy a car, you're mad at everybody who's ahead of you because you've got to get there first! Like those people constantly changing lanes on the freeway, almost killing people—just to get there five seconds faster. Or you're on a plane and the pilot comes on the radio: "Takeoff will be delayed due to mechanical problems . . ." Everybody freaks: "Oh, no, none of these delays now . . ." Banging on the cockpit door: "Open up! Get this plane rolling!"

"But, sir, the wings are falling off . . ."

"Too bad! The passengers have voted. We're not waiting another second!"

Speed addiction is behind just about every stupid problem we have. Like crime: Who tries to rob you with a knife anymore? Nobody—you'd bust out laughing: "Sorry, man, it's not you I'm laughing at, it's the knife. Now I'm gonna run away and let's see if you can catch me and get my money."

No way—a real thug's got to have a gun, and not just any gun. It's got to be a semi- or fully automatic— "I don't have time to keep pulling this trigger with my finger . . . I'm in a hurry. I need your money!"

Speaking of guns, I know the NRA keeps saying that every man and woman has the right to bear arms to protect their family. But I think that law was written when things were just a little wilder, when your nearest neighbor was 200 miles away and it could take you thirty minutes to load a bullet. If they knew you could get an Uzi or an AK-47 fully automatic assault rifle, they might have phrased that law a little differently: "A man has the right to bear a *musket* . . ."

For all you hunters out there, what kind of animals are you killing with hand grenades and assault rifles? I saw that movie *Night of the Giant Thumpers*, about giant killer rabbits, but I just didn't know they were real.

The solution? Force every person over the age of seven to own a fully automatic weapon and carry it with him at all times. Then we'll have to fight to get those guns into people's homes. They'll find some way to justify not having weapons. America wants only what it can't have.

Another problem that comes from speed addiction: fast food, like McDonald's. There's a whole generation of American children who don't even know that humans once cooked their food in pots on the stove

("Oh, maybe back in the Stone Age, Daddy—I saw it on *The Flintstones*") or ordered it from waiters off leather menus in restaurants with candles and flowers on the tables. Fast food is all they know.

And it's not fast enough. Guy ahead of you in line at McDonald's is staring at the list of ten choices: "Hmm . . . I wonder what's good?"

There goes your patience! "Hey, Jack, the menu hasn't changed in your last one hundred visits!"

Takes twenty minutes for them to hand him some kind of bag to shake him, then you're up: "Give me a fish sandwich and a chocolate shake." Before you get busy with that chocolate shake—look out! There's not a man alive who ever sucked a McDonald's shake up through the straw. They use that thin kind of straw on purpose, just to watch your face collapse. Give it a mighty suck—*ummffff*—eyeballs be bulging out of your head, veins in your brain about to bust unless you pass out first. Those shakes are thick! You'll never get the strength to finish. That's not fast food! Or else they give you one of those broken straws so air comes in and it pops in your face.

And check this out: There's no more numbers on the cash register keys at McDonald's—just pictures of the food. *Ka-ching, ka-ching*—get your change—"What's up, man? You charged me for a burger when I said a fish sandwich."

"No, I charged you for the chicken, sir. All those keys just look the same."

And when the automatic change-maker isn't working, forget it. I gave one kid a five-dollar bill—my total came to $4.95. He's going, "Umm . . . umm . . .

ummm . . . sir, why don't you just reach in and take what you think is right?"

The slowest part of any fast-food restaurant is the drive-up "express" window. Whoever came up with that term ought to be smacked silly. Express—maybe the pony express window. You'd probably get through faster on a horse. The guy with the little headphones on can't hear you—"You want what?"—his ears are bleeding from all the screaming. Your friends in the back are yelling: "Get me a Big Mac and a Pepsi!" "Bzzzzztttttt"—you translate, "No Pepsi, just Coke." "Arch Deluxe with bacon, double fries, orange pop." "Sausage biscuit!" "Blagabagazzzzz"—"Too late, breakfast stops at eleven." "Okay, Mountain Dew instead of Pepsi." "Crakackack"—"No orange, just Coke." "Double fries with the sausage biscuit." "ZZZZZakkkk"—"No Mountain Dew, just Coke. No sausage biscuit." You're about to lose your mind. "Give me a double cheeseburger!"

"Pull over"—loud and clear.

"Why?"

"The double-cheese guy is on break."

"Huh?" Only one guy can slap some meat on three hunks of bun, like it's a science; y'all got this factory line where people only learn one job?—"Sorry, I'm not trained on that one yet."

He hands you a beeper: "I've got to special order it and beep you when it's ready."

You pull over, parking next to a car all rusted out and full of skeletons. The folks behind you try to warn you, shaking their fingers, "Don't go out there—that food will never come." Then you hear *bleep, bleep!*

Beeper's going off in the dead folks' car. "Hey—their food is ready. Let's get it!"

Why not? Who ever gets the food they ordered anyway? Like the apple pie, it's never in the bag—y'all can't believe we really want it. But what's weird is no one ever checks the bag before they leave—like they've been hypnotized: "I will drive nine miles back in the snow for the McNuggets . . ."

I don't even order anymore when I go to McDonald's. I just say, "Y'all surprise me like you always do . . ."

My advice: When you go to a fast-food place, make it a game. Drive real fast to the pickup window before the guy tells you how much it costs. That upsets them.

One of the worst things about speed addiction is how we want an instant fix for everything. If you tell them, "Hey, you've got to pay some dues, got to take time to work things out," they just shout back, "I'm gone."

All this I-got-to-have-it-quick attitude makes TV dangerous, especially after midnight. It can possess you. How else can you explain a 400-pound guy flipping through the channels and there's an infomercial, one of those ab isolators, flatten your stomach in twenty days—and actually buying it, like it's going to happen? Or the psychic network comes on—nine o'clock at night: "How could anyone be so stupid?" Four o'clock in the morning: "Man, I need a quick fix; let's see if these psychics really work." Wake one up at four A.M. —how do you know she's not a little off? And if she's not asleep, you got to wonder: "If you're so psychic, why can't you see your way to a better life than sitting by the phone all night long?" We have all called a psychic hotline one time. But if you call again, you're possessed. You're sinking down to rehab level.

And what about those talk shows? Like our problems can be solved in one hour on a TV talk show . . . People go on, tell a story, an expert gives the answer—some woman been divorced five times, working on her sixth, telling us how to have a good relationship. Ladies, first of all, let's be careful—never take advice from a woman who doesn't have somebody. You think she wants you to be happy? Would you let a snaggle-toothed dentist work on your teeth?

Men, if you get invited to go on one of those shows and they put you in the soundproof booth, don't come out. Don't sit down in that chair next to your woman. Are you stupid enough to think they're going to cheer you on? No, they want to dog you! That girl you thought nobody knew about is waiting for you behind the curtain. *Boom*—here she comes! That's why they put you in the soundproof booth, stupid!

Half the stories on those shows aren't even real. I know this for sure because I know my people. No black woman would go on a show with her husband who got somebody else pregnant and calmly ask him questions: "What do you have to say for yourself?" No black man would sit on that chair between those women while they're asking those questions—"You think I'm crazy? You think I wanna die?" No way that man could be alive on TV—we better put him in the witness protection program.

The talk show host I respect the most is Oprah. She can find the Dead Sea Scrolls, and every woman in the country will say, "Yeah, I always wanted to read those. Oprah said it's hard, but stick with it . . ." Oprah taught women to walk in the light and be themselves— I'm down with that—but things have never been the same for men.

Most of those shows make men look like dogs, deadbeats, and no-good daddies. But now and then we get one that makes guys look good. There was one show that really touched me; it was about "makeovers for men"—like, if you respect your woman, you'll try to look good for her. They had before and after: First they show this guy in overalls, raggedy old boots and cap, then they bring him out in an eighty-dollar haircut and a thousand-dollar suit. All the women start whistling and clapping, "Whoo, now there's a man! Turn around so I can get the back view . . ." And the guy just stands there. He's crying: "I can't buy suits like this. I have a normal job, I work on cars. I didn't know you were ashamed of me."

His wife just freaked: "Put my man back in his old clothes. Baby, I love you just the way you are . . ." And the host did the right thing—turned the show around to talk about what's important: Does the man work hard all day? Does he come home and take care of his family? That's what you got to think about.

Men, we need a new show of our own, let's face it— an *Oprah* show for men. Until we get one, Oprah should have a service: Give her the fax number of every man in America so every day, automatically, she can fax us the transcripts of her show so we know what to expect when we get home. For the more technologically minded, there could be a Web site so we could download the transcripts daily from anywhere in the world. Oprahize us, I'm begging you, so we can keep up with our women!

WWW.Com, or The Wild, Wild West Is Back Again

Now, how about all this new technology: those answering machines and computers, VCRs that program you to watch them, E-mail, DSS, DBS, DBD, BVD—no, that's underwear; that's a different chapter. We thought technology would bring us freedom, but it's done the opposite. It started with answering machines. We wanted them so we wouldn't miss those one or two important calls—the *one or two*, not the seventy-five calls you've got waiting for you now, all saying the same thing: "What's up, man? Call me back"; not even leaving the phone number! And it's getting worse: Everybody's got a beeper now. One show I did, a sister's beeper kept going off, loud. "All those calls, miss— that's some stressful job you got. Are you a doctor?" No, she's a beautician. Ten o'clock at night—what emergency could come up? How many people get their hair done at ten o'clock at night? "Oh, it's late, I know, but it's urgent—I got to get some naps relaxed!" Even jobless, homeless people got beepers. This dude with a shopping cart was asking me for spare change—*Beep!* Can you believe this? His beeper went off! Now, who would be beeping a homeless dude? Somebody with some spare change looking for him?

When folks beep you, you almost kill yourself getting off the highway to a phone. "Whew—what's up? Everything okay?"

"Hey, man . . . I was just calling to see what you were doing."

"What am I doing? What am I doing? I'm driving over to your house to jack you up is what I'm doing! Go stand out on the sidewalk until I get there, wasting my time like that." Like it doesn't matter you got scared half to death—they've got to talk to you when they want to. But a few times like that, you get a cellular phone—and pretty soon, you are never alone.

I would bet money it's women who invented this technology so men can't hide anymore. In the good old days, you could go where you wanted. No one could find you till you felt like calling in, and you could lie: "Hi, baby. Yes, I'm still at the office. What music? Oh, it's just the radio keeping me company." But now you can't get away with that—they've got this star 69, star 66, and caller ID to reveal your location. You can't say, "I've been trying to reach you"—she's got an answering machine; or "The line was busy"—call waiting put a stop to that.

There are those radio transmitters to trace stolen cars—just wait a couple of years till that technology gets cheaper and we'll all be wearing personal trackers on our bodies. Teenagers won't be able to hide from their parents anymore—"Oh, I know where you were, I know what party you were at. I can track it!" Parents will zap you with 10,000 volts of electricity to make you come home, blast you on the giant speakers attached to your body, embarrass you in front of all your friends. There will be constant surveillance.

Maybe that's good, but it's scary, man—the stuff we think of as toys are tools taking control of our lives. Look at computers—there's this new group of people, the digerati, they call them, who are like "I never use a pen"; they're the guys you see on the plane—whip out the computer and jam on the keys the whole trip. When I get on a plane with my kids and I see one of them glare like "Keep them quiet. This is my office," I say, "Son, I'm going to sleep. That guy has a nice computer you can play with. Go ahead and jack it up." Hey, who are these guys, trying to act like they're so important, got to work on the plane? They probably don't even have jobs, just nice suits and good computers—trying to fake the funk. I'm not buying it. And I can't understand folks who won't even read a magazine unless it's on-screen—how can you give up your freedom to move around? And where do you put your laptop when you're reading on the toilet? That must be some kind of balancing act!

Computers used to be these plain beige boxes, but now we want ones that look slick. I love how people go to the store and say, "I want a state-of-the-art computer for doing my taxes and keeping my accounts," when, unless you're a developing nation, all you need is $100 worth of software. Salesmen love to sucker those folks, sending them home with multimedia machines that do three-dimensional drawings, play music, make movies —what for, man? Who's really editing their family videos; adding background music and jazzing them up with some animation—"The dog had died, but we loved him, so I scanned in Lassie." "It was really a station wagon but I retouched it into a Ferrari . . ." "Honey, we have to put the sound track on this video: the O'Jays' 'Family Reunion.'" Who is really doing this stuff?

Let's face it: Do you even use the address book or calendar on your computer? Make a date for Saturday: "Whoa, Whitney, just let me fire up the laptop—oops, battery's low, I better plug it in; let me just crawl under the table now. Uh-huh, turning it on. Give me your home number, baby—*tictictictic*—no, I'm not typing yet, it's just booting up—let's see, click on the apple, go to . . . Whitney, are you there?" No way can you just write it down on a scrap of paper—no, you've got to use the new technology. Got to justify that $2,000 address book!

Now, don't get me wrong—I dig the new technology. I've been known to fall asleep while chatting on-line at five or six in the morning. But here's what I really want: a computer that can scan in all my stuff, then when I need something I can type in "black socks, clean," or "car keys," and it will spit them out. Now, that would be a big help, man.

And this Internet thing is a trip. I got on it from the jump—back then there were only maybe twenty of us in the whole country; and nobody made any sense:

Starchild to Moon Man: Hi.

Moon Man to Starchild: Hi, Mac or PC?

Starchild: IBM 1370, XYZ, 1.6 megahertz, 12 gigabytes, loaded with . . .

Moon Man: Mac SE, 9 RAM, hypercard with . . .

That's how I spent most of the 1980s. Hey, even the name they came up with, the information superhighway, is dumb. I think www stands more for "wild, wild West" than World Wide Web. That's what it's like—a big desert with all these people riding through it in their little covered wagons, covered so you don't know who they are, far from civilization so they can act as crazy as they want to. You don't want to be a cowboy out there meeting them alone on your horse.

That's why chatting on-line is so scary. You've got some 6'5" foul-smelling hairy men pretending to be 5'4" voluptuous women. I mean, think about it—anybody who's on-line at four or five in the morning can't have much of a life. I think that's when serial killers and other nuts are up planning their next jobs. I think Charles Manson would have his own Web page if he were free—or maybe he does: "Hi, I'm Samantha. I'm kind of tied up right now. I'd like to meet you in about seventy-five years. Signed, *Charles*—cr, uh—*Samantha.*"

Real people—they call them "fleshies"—can't compete with these cyberfolks. People get so addicted to being on-line—you see folks walking the streets with a telephone cord; they come to your house, knock on the door—"Hey, can I plug in to your phone?"

"Why? Are you lonely? You want to talk? You can talk to me."

"No, I can't talk to anyone I can see, man. Hook me up."

Look, it's okay to have your computers, your Wizards, your Psions—but keep that ink pen and pad of paper handy. I've got a feeling that we'll be needing them for a long time to come.

Just Say No

What is it about a person not drinking or getting high that makes people who do so nervous? They keep acting like they're worried about you, like you have a problem. It is a constant test: "You don't get high, you don't drink—what do you do for fun?"

"Well, let's see—I guess I just watch you tear around like a fool, and when I get a chance, I trip you up. That's what's fun to me." I guarantee you that will mess with a person's high.

After a while people stop trying to make you drink and realize that they can make you their designated driver, which can be a hilarious job. In my early days as a comic, when we drove to all our gigs instead of flying, I babysat many a drunk, and I came to enjoy it. If you're playing the job straight, you'll get folks' addresses while they are sober because there's nothing worse than trying to find drunk people's houses. You'll be turning down every street because they have no clue where they live.

But if you take my lighthearted approach to the job, you'll see that addresses don't matter—you can drop off drunk people anywhere. You can drop them off at McDonald's: "I think this is your house." They will get out saying, "Oh, man, I left all the lights on."

When I was in college (before I realized it was cool enough just being myself) I'd tell the other guys crazy lies about what I'd done while I was drunk to explain why I had sobered up. Some of my stuff was really good —I'm a first-class liar—like the story where I passed out, drove into the river, and had to swim ashore. But I am glad to say that the truth is that I have never puked on myself, walked through a glass door and not felt it until the morning, used the bathroom on myself, used the bathroom on someone else, lost my car and never found it again, or woke up with a whole marching band lying in my bed next to me.

Men like to brag about acting crazy when they are drunk: "And I smashed the car right into the window of the bank; alarms screaming, I swear . . ." But no matter how crazy men act when they get drunk, there's nothing scarier than a drunken woman. When women get drunk they want to stay out all night and be loud and embarrass you.

You say, "Baby, let's go."

"I'M NOT READY TO GO! I AM HAVING FUN. YOU JUST HATE IT WHEN I HAVE FUN!"

Some women even get violent. They will box everybody in the room, and win.

Here's my suggestion for any man who is out with a woman who gets drunk: Leave her there and go home. The next morning tell her that you dropped her off at her house but that she must have walked back to the party. Don't worry—she won't remember a thing. You hope! Women, you don't have to worry about a drunken man. He will walk home on his own because he will never find his car keys. I think when men get drunk, all their keys jump out of their pockets so they can finally be free. That's just a theory, I can't prove it.

Now, marijuana is a different kind of high. One thing you don't have to worry about when people smoke pot is fights—it is physically impossible to fight when high on pot. And people can't drive either: They think they are flying—the speedometer doesn't even move. When the police try to come after them, they have to get out of the car and walk to catch up to the potheads —no regular driver can go that slow. Here's a tip: If a pothead tries to give you a ride home, just say no. You'll get there quicker if you walk or catch the bus.

And how about this old line: "I use drugs because they open up my mind. I do my best work when I am high." Yeah, right, they open your mind, all right—and let out what little sense you had. Your brains fall right out on the floor. In the seventies people started experimenting with all kinds of weird chemicals. When I was twelve and working at the local mom and pop corner store, these teenagers kept coming in to buy gallons of Bactine. I thought somebody must have been in a bad accident and didn't have insurance. I later found out that they were getting high—high on *Bactine*. If you're getting high on Bactine, you know you're desperate or you need a better job. At least if you OD'd on Bactine you wouldn't hurt.

Then what I call the dummy drugs came in—drugs with goofy names like LSD, PCP, XTC—that made you go straight to stupid. Nothing like putting embalming fluid into a live body for a test run. Or how about some horse tranquilizer: "Strong enough to stop a horse, I need some of that, yum, yum."

I remember once a friend of mine in college started screaming, "Get them! Somebody help me, please get them."

I thought somebody was hurting my man. I came running into the room, but when I realized he was just tripping, I decided to have some fun. I asked, "Get what?"

He said, "My legs, they ran out of the room, man."

So I took off to chase his legs, then I came back to break the sad news—"Hey, man, I'm sorry. They got hit by a car." He had to roll down the hall to his bedroom, that's how much he believed me.

The next day he saw me and said, "Very funny. You know I was high. You shouldn't have done that to me."

And I had to say, "I couldn't help myself. You were too easy."

During my freshman year in college, I witnessed the impossible: a student on drugs skiing down the side of the dormitory. I was in the eighth-floor lounge watching *Star Trek* when this guy—wearing all his ski equipment and talking about his destiny—proceeded to tie a rope to the couch leg, with the other end around his waist. He asked me for my help. Since I had never skied a day in my life, I thought he might be doing something normal, even when he got up on the window ledge and, pointing at me, jumped, yelling, "Dudeeeeeeeeeeeeeeeeeeeeeee." I have to admit he looked good for about four seconds while he was skiing; he fell the rest of the way. He impressed me so much that I vowed to learn to ski, only on snow.

But he was lucky: I saw him in the spring walking around like Herman Munster in a body cast. He had survived when a sober man would have died, just from knowing how jacked up he was. I think the drugs saved his life. When I told him who I was, he asked, "Why didn't you stop me?" Well, I had to say, "I thought you knew something I didn't."

I am glad I finally started taking pride in the fact that I don't get high and try to do the right things in life. I mean, come on—my father is a minister and my mother is a Christian; they're not going to play when it comes to their kids doing the right things in life. My dad taught me that being "good" doesn't make you weak—in fact, it means you are stronger. He showed me that the Bible was full of tough dudes. Samson, for example, killed a thousand people, killed a lion with his bare hands—you going to call him a sissy? Delilah did kick his butt pretty good, but that was a case of entrapment. How about Joshua at the battle of Jericho? He was a down militant, played the horn (I think it was a saxophone). He was strong enough to handle ridicule and insurrection when God told him to walk around Jericho blowing his horn rather than look cool in front of his men throwing a spear at the enemy. He waited for the word from above and then they went in and took care of business.

The morals of this story: 1. Before you do any drugs in your life, watch somebody else do that drug first and see how stupid he acts. 2. Don't get high around me because I will have some fun. And—last but not least —3. Don't mistake meekness for weakness.

Afros, Bell-Bottoms, and Silk Boxers

I've never been cool.

After I saw *Superfly*, I wanted to be a pimp. The problem was that I was only thirteen. I didn't have a woman yet, and I couldn't wait to go get a fake fur coat. No woman, no cool clothes, just a wannabe pimp—on a bicycle.

Now, I wouldn't have made too cool a pimp since my father is a preacher and I was raised right. I would have been the first *nice* pimp in the world. I probably would have *lent* money to my girls instead of *taking* money from them. I would have given pimping a bad name.

That shows you the power of movies. We finally had black people on the screen. But hey, even though I might not have made a cool pimp, you cannot argue with me about this—to this day, to me, there is no cool like seventies cool. If you gave me the keys to a time machine, you wouldn't have to put much gas in the tank, because I would go no farther back than the seventies. To me it was the coolest decade ever.

Yeah, I know what I'm talking about—I survived the seventies and the seventies taught us everything we needed to know. The seventies took it to the limit. We went crazy in the seventies. After the seventies, everything seemed calm.

The seventies were when guys wore silk underwear that hung out underneath their gym trunks. The coolest guys would have silk underwear in three different colors. These guys were getting clothes from BB's, a store in my hometown where you also bought silk socks and double-knit pants. I used to stand in front of that store, thinking, "One day I'll be wearing silk."

Well, one day Mom went to a rummage sale and found me some silk briefs. I know what you are thinking, "You didn't put on somebody else's used underwear, did you?" Not to worry, I washed them in hot water and Lysol, FIVE TIMES. They were fire-engine red and vomit green. Not exactly what I was looking for. But they were better than nothing and it wasn't like I had a string of silkworms at my beck and call to spin out my custom order. Since they were briefs they weren't long enough to hang below my gym shorts. And that meant no one would know I was wearing silk shorts. I would whisper to my friends, "You can't tell by looking, but I am wearing silk underwear." I lost a lot of my friends after doing that. Now that I think about it, I must have sounded like some kind of weirdo.

The coolest cats in the seventies were the basketball

players and the coolest player of all was Walt Frazier, the New York Knick known as "Clyde." Clyde had super-thick sideburns that got wider as they got longer. On the streets of New York City he wore a big white fur coat and a wide-brimmed mack daddy hat. He looked like a pimp with a jump shot. I was so into Clyde that I took Mom's eyebrow pencil and drew sideburns on my face. I'd look cool until I would start sweating and then I looked like Bozo the Clown on acid.

My Afro was vintage seventies, big and red. In the seventies, there was no such thing as an Afro being too big. Afros were political. To be a strong black leader, you needed an Afro. If you couldn't grow an Afro at least five to six inches, your activist career was shot. Before the meetings, brothers measured their Afros. The brother with the biggest Afro led the meeting. Of course, the best Afro would be a wavy-hair Afro. We called that the good hair look. Black was beautiful, but wavy black was even more beautiful.

Some bros and sisses had Afros so big you couldn't see their faces underneath the 'fro. You didn't know who was coming down the street. You would think it was a fine sister until they said something, then you had to recover, "Oh, yeah, Tommy, how you doing?"

The coolest TV show in the seventies was *Soul Train*. Everyone from the Midwest wanted to be on *Soul Train* so we could meet what we thought were the finest girls in the universe. Of course the sisters thought LA brothers were the finest because of their Afros. If someone in my town had a relative come visit from LA with one of those LA 'fros, the girls would go crazy over the brother—even if he had a pizza face and weighed only 120 pounds. The "LA 'Fro" was it. Everyone on

Soul Train had like wonder Afros. We figured that was because they used the Afro Sheen blow-up kits advertised on the show. But the Afro Sheen blow-up kits didn't always blow up. In the real world outside *Soul Train*, we had sorry-looking, limpy, lumpy Afros, Afros sagging on the side or the back or worst of all, the flatback 'fro—an afro that was perfectly round except in the back. It was just flat. There must be some scientific reason for this strange phenomenon. Why else would your 'fro be seven inches high everywhere else and only two inches in the back. You had to make sure that when rapping to women you never turned around, lest they see you were a flat-back brother. Guaranteed to kill any chances of a date.

If Afros couldn't be too big in the seventies, stack heels couldn't be too high, hip huggers couldn't be too tight, and a guy's shirt couldn't show too much chest. In the seventies, you wanted to look like a walking exclamation point. You had to have a concave chest. It was important that your chest actually meet your back so that if you stood sideways you could disappear in the crowd. Nobody worked out in the seventies, nobody was buffed. Being scrawny was cool.

Those bell-bottoms were something. Men tried to squeeze themselves into the tightest pants they could stand, and then the pants would flare out to the bells at the bottom. The bells got so big they could be dangerous. While you were dancing, at any moment your bells could whip around and wrap up somebody else's feet and take them down. There were a few short guys who disappeared from the dance floor mysteriously in the seventies. We were convinced that they were just swept up in someone's bell-bottoms never to be heard from again.

There will never be bad taste like the bad taste of the seventies. I was a prime example. My dad would take me to Chicago to shop for my school clothes at Smokey Joe's, a super-hip clothing store. That's where I got my white fake fur coat with matching hat. It looked like the coat the character Goldie wore in the movie *The Mack,* another pimp movie from the seventies (pimps were very big in the seventies). These were the coolest things I owned other than the purple and black jumpsuit my mother made for me. The coat looked good until the first snowstorm. That's when it started shedding, fake fur flying off me like chicken feathers.

In the seventies, you could never wear a color too bright or in the wrong combination. Everything went with everything. You could never wear too much makeup. Now, in the nineties, we have a thing about good taste. Everyone wants good taste. Soft, off-white, subtle designer gray. I hate that. In the seventies, there was no such thing as good taste. Everything was loud and obnoxious, the way life should be

We couldn't get enough of the seventies blacksploitation movies like *Superfly* and *The Mack.* They showed black life in the big city like it had never been seen on the screen before. I especially loved *The Mack.* Seeing *The Mack* and hearing Willie Hutch's funky score had me in a macked-out fever. The funny thing is I didn't smoke dope, drink alcohol, or even have girlfriends. It was just the Mack style that appealed to me.

I bought mailbox letters—mailbox letters!—and spelled out T-H-E M-A-C-K on the side of our beat-up 1965 Impala. My brother Michael used the car once and came home complaining, "What is a Mack?" because people were laughing at him whenever he got out of the car. Now Michael was the opposite of me. He was a classical pianist and a genius student. When I told him what a mack was, he was less than pleased. "Mom," he said, "look what it says on the side of the car." Mom had no idea that a mack was a pimp. She thought Mack was the name of an NBA player. I never had to share that car with Michael ever again.

I was not fazed. I added on those outsized whitewalls, the kind that were all show and no go. Completing the package were a dozen speakers I stole from the drive-in movie where I worked weekends, in addition to two giant speakers from the home stereo center I stuck in the backseat.

Yes, I was all macked out and I still couldn't get a girl. My love life had more in common with Johnny Quest than Superfly, but at least I was a funky Johnny Quest.

What I wanted was a woman like Pam Grier. We had never seen a woman like Pam Grier. She was Coffy and Foxy Brown and Sheba Baby. Was she ever! She was a fantasy so sexy and tough and larger than life, certainly than any life we were leading. We watched those Pam Grier movies with our mouths open and our eyes wide. Pam was our queen.

I also liked Ron O'Neal, who was Superfly. His hair was long and wavy and superslick and I wanted hair just like it. When I tried it, though, I wound up looking like Moms Mabley.

But it is the music of the seventies that has had the most lasting impact on me. And judging from the wild crowds we get at the "Sinbad's '70s Summer Jam" concerts we've done with HBO on Memorial Day for the past three years, there's a mess of people who agree.

That's because there's no funk like seventies funk. It fired me up. I thought bands like Earth, Wind & Fire came down from Jupiter just to lay it on us. It wasn't just funk, it was far-out funk. The first time I heard Ohio Players' "Funky Worm" I was driving our macked-up Impala. The funk was so fat I had to pull over to the side of the road. My heart started hammering in time to the beat. I broke out in a cold sweat. I drove over to Avery's Record Store, which was just some dude selling albums—yes, wax: there's a seventies term that you won't hear in the CD nineties—out of his garage. I played my single of "Funky Worm" so much I actually wore down the grooves.

Of course, the in-car music format that was pure seventies was the eight-track tape player. Kids today don't have to wait for anything. They've got CD players, and they can jump, jump, jump from song to song, back and forth. We had eight-tracks. You haven't lived until you've had an eight-track. I think eight-tracks were the reason why the albums were so good in the seventies. The whole album had to grab you because the eight-track machines had no fast-forward or rewind buttons. You had to listen to the whole album. And if you wanted to hear a particular song again, you had to stay in the car and ride around until the whole tape played through. That was your fast-forward, you kept riding around until the song came back up. There are a few potheads from the seventies who still swear that if you rode around in reverse the tape would rewind.

Between really deep geniuses like Curtis Mayfield and Marvin Gaye and madmen like Bootsie Collins and George Clinton, the funk was kicking. Every band seemed to have one mandatory guy who hit the wood block. He had no skills, except that he wore love beads and tie-dyed shirts and banged the wood block. He didn't even seem to hit the wood block on time. I myself was a drummer. The bad thing about playing the drums is nobody (girls) could see you when the band was playing. They would think you were lying to them when you tried to talk to them after the show: "Ooh, girl, this fool thinks he is in the band." Thanks to my seventies music, I am now, and hope to always be, still funked up after all these years.

I don't have any advice for you in this chapter. I just love the seventies so much I had to put all this stuff in.

Ironing My Pants

I was reading in the paper the other day an article about "style." They talked about Michael Jordan, Bill Cosby, Tiger Woods, Toni Braxton, and Al Pacino, to name a few. I realized that all these people had something that defined them, made them original, and was inimitable. For example, you can hang your tongue out of your mouth like Michael Jordan, but it is not the same. It belongs to him and him alone. As they say, "Often imitated, never duplicated."

So I started thinking about what my style is. And I couldn't find that one thing that stood out. I don't make any special facial expressions. How about my hair? Nope, Dennis Rodman does it better. Then I started panicking. Every entertainer needs a style.

So I started keeping a journal on everything I did during the day to help me find my style. I paid particularly close attention to my performing habits, both off- and onstage, in the dressing room before a show, looking for my signature mannerisms or actions. I thought, "Do I sweat a special way, say, *glistening* as opposed to *slimey*?" Definitely slimey, but that is not style, that's just funk.

So I started watching other comics to check out their style, not that I was going to copy anybody, although I do like Cosby's chair technique. Maybe I could work it into my act, just change the type of chair—maybe a couch? No, too big. I got it, a love seat? No, maybe too sexual for the kids. A barstool? Nope, too drug-related. Aw, forget the chair, I don't want to sit down anyway.

A lot of comedians are finicky about their routines, both their comedy routines that they perform onstage and their pre-performance routines that get them psyched-up to go out and be funny in front of an audience. Many of these comics follow the same set of jokes night after night to the letter, and if a heckler interrupts them it can throw off their entire show. Similarly, if they skip a step in their superstitious back-stage rituals before the show, it can mess up their whole night.

Of course, add to this the fact that comedians are entertainers, which means they start from a base of being neurotic, driven, hyper, jealous, and plain crazy. And that's on their good days.

I even tried to invent some kind of ritual before going onstage. For a while I tried meditating. It didn't work, I would get headaches and hyperventilate. I now know you're not supposed to hold your breath while doing it. Then I tried chanting but kept forgetting the words—NE NAKAHATCHI REMKAY YO YO, or something like that—and people thought I was talking gibberish. "Have you seen Sinbad lately, he's starting to trip out. I heard him talking to himself in some strange language before the show."

I even started eating strange foods before going on-stage. Stuff like crawfish, Rocky Mountain oysters (I swear I didn't know what they were), and eggplant. I was trying to be exotic. Didn't work, though; just gave me gas. Lost an agent and a personal assistant over that one. I watched other comics write their material down. I never write down the material I'm going to perform. I like to hit the stage and just run with whatever is on my mind, and I love to play with the audience and get them involved in the show. It's a different adventure every night. When I started writing things down, I kept losing the paper.

After many disappointments I gave up. Then it happened. One night I was running late to a gig and Mark, my brother/manager, said, "Are you ready to go on?"

"No, I have to iron my pants."

He said, "You always have to iron your pants right before a show, what's up with that?"

IRON MY PANTS!

That's it. That is my style. It was staring me right in the face and I never saw it. I am known for ironing my pants, and strutting my great creases. HA HA.

I'm ready to laugh at life and challenge fools—that's the spirit I loved in the original Sinbad. I refuse to get all rabbity with fears and doubts. I've failed at so many things in my life, one more is not going to tip me over. And if things ever threaten to get too dull, I'll go looking for new adventures. Have iron, will travel, ready for whatever I find, and having a sharp crease when I get there.

I have reached this simple focus after years of scrambling around trying to find my path in life. They were hard years, Jack, full of wild adventures, with my share of suffering and more than my share of laughs along the way. Which is pretty much all I ever wanted out of life, to be allowed the opportunity to make people laugh. Even if I had known back at the beginning how difficult the journey would be, I still would not have wanted to pick any other path.

I have my parents to thank for allowing me to choose this crazy life and for always supporting my actions, no matter how doubtful they may have been about how I was progressing. I want to send a special shout out to my mother for teaching me how to iron and the secret of great creases—two parts white vinegar and one part water put in a spray bottle and then get your daddy's used (handles heat better) handkerchief to use as a pressing cloth.

A lot of parents would have long ago insisted, "Get a real job! Kroger's is hiring" (although I don't think this "thieving child" could get a job there). But my mother and father always pushed me to keep looking for *my* laughs, *my* way.

Yes, the reason I am what I am today is because I had a mother and father who cared enough to keep me in line, but who also always allowed me to dream my dreams.

And I want to thank all my brothers and sisters for thinking my being a comic was the coolest thing in the world.

I also have to thank my kids, Paige and Royce, for not being embarrassed to be seen with the ol' man.

Mama, Daddy, thank you. Even the original Sinbad didn't have parents as cool as you.

And I know he didn't have as sharp a crease in his pants as I do.

About the Authors

Born in Benton Harbor, Michigan, Sinbad grew up telling jokes to his three brothers and two sisters. They are very glad he's finally out of the house. Not as glad as his parents, though.

He costarred with Arnold Schwarzenegger in *Jingle All the Way*, and he was the star of *House Guest, First Kid*, and the HBO film *The Cherokee Kid*. His enormously successful HBO Comedy Specials have included *Brain Damaged* and *Son of a Preacher Man*.

David Ritz has written books with Marvin Gaye, Ray Charles, Smokey Robinson, B.B. King, and Etta James. His lyrics include "Sexual Healing"; his novels include *The Man Who Brought the Dodgers Back to Brooklyn*.